"EARTH

AND ALL THE

STARS..."

Reconnecting with Nature through Hymns, Stories, Poems, and Prayers from the World's Great Religions and Cultures

Edited by

Anne Rowthorn

New World Library
Novato, California

New World Library
14 Pamaron Way
Novato, California 94949

Copyright © 2000 by Anne Rowthorn
Edited by Gina Misiroglu and Katharine Farnam Conolly
Cover and text design: Mary Ann Casler

Library of Congress Cataloging-in-Publication Data
Rowthorn, Anne
Earth and all the stars: reconnecting with nature through hymns, stories, poems, and prayers from the world's great religions and cultures / Anne Rowthorn.
p. cm.
ISBN: 1-57731-106-x (perfect)
I. Human ecology — Religious aspects. 2. Meditations. I. Title.
GF80.R69 2000
291.4'32—dc21   99-049439

First Printing, March 2000
ISBN 1-57731-106-x
Printed in Canada on acid-free paper
Distributed to the trade by Publishers Group West
10 9 8 7 6 5 4 3 2 1

Of the multitude
     of bright stars
     in the universe,
     only one
     am I privileged
     to call

     MUM

Thank you
     for
     life,
     light,
     laughter,
     love.

Always.

Table of Contents

ACKNOWLEDGMENTS

No one compiles a book of this nature without the help of many, people known and unknown. Primarily, I would like to acknowledge my gratitude to all the authors of every age whose material forms the substance of *Earth and All the Stars*. Grateful thanks are due to the students who have participated in my Caring for Creation course at the Hartford Seminary in Connecticut. It was with them that the idea of this project originated and where some of the material was tested and adapted. Paris, where I live, is rich in resources of all kinds and wonderful libraries. I am grateful to the extremely helpful reference librarians at the the following Parisian libraries: National Library of the Georges Pompidou Center, the Inter-University Library of Oriental Languages, and the American Library (a part of the American University in Paris).

The goodwill of many copyright holders facilitated the compilation of this book. Several reduced or waived their fees. Permissions editors, too, were of tremendous assistance, responding to my requests and aiding me in identifying copyright holders. Special thanks are due to the following authors, agents, organizations, and publishers who generously donated their works free of charge: Diane Ackerman; Moyra Caldecott; Matthew Fox; Thich Nhat Hanh; Robert O'Rourke; Peter Gold; Helen S. Maurer; Peace Child International; Kurama Temple in Kyoto, Japan; John Pairman Brown; World Council of Churches; Martin Palmer; David Adam; Worldwide Fund for Nature; Harvard University Press; Don DiVecchio; HarperCollins, Ltd. London; Jeffery Rowthorn; the Hymn Society; the Benedictine Foundation of the State of Vermont Inc.; Kate Compston; United Nations Environmental Programe; SYNDESMOS; the World Fellowship of

Orthodox Youth; Wild Goose Publications (Iona Community); *Maryknoll Magazine;* the Anglican Church of Aotearoa, New Zealand, and Polynesia; and the Council of Churches for Britain and Ireland.

I am grateful for all the interest and assistance given me by Karen Gallagher of Greenpeace International in Amsterdam; the artist, Jane Hooker, a special friend of this project; my son, Christian Rowthorn, who opened the door to the spiritual treasures of Japan for me; and many others such as Kenyon Cull, Judith Conley, and Mark Maryboy, who sent relevant material, led me to it, or explained its significance.

I most heartily thank my editor, Gina Misiroglu, of New World Library. No one could have asked for a more helpful and attentive editor. Her creativity and clear vision have greatly enhanced the presentation of this book.

Finally, my husband, Jeffery Rowthorn, has encouraged and lived with this project since its inception — not easy to do in a small city apartment with source books and drafts everywhere. He bore with it and in addition offered innumerable practical suggestions. For this and all his love and support I am immensely grateful.

INTRODUCTION

Earth is crammed with heaven,
and every common bush afire with God,
but only those who see
take off their shoes.

— *Elizabeth Barrett Browning*

"There is a true yearning to respond to the singing river and the wise rock," as Maya Angelou so eloquently reminded us in her poem entitled "On the Pulse of the Morning." The singing river calls us to sit on her banks and to heed her call to wake up to the beauty of God's creation. The stinking garbage piled six feet high on Tirana's main street, the foul, polluted air of midtown Manhattan, the clear-cutting of a Brazilian rain forest call us to repentance. The fresh green pastures of Ireland, the purple mountains of Wyoming, the waving Kansas wheat fields, the dove call at dawn, the wind-song of a crisp March day summon us to a new day of love and gratitude, of care and healing for God's creation. This is the time to wake up to the new day, the time to plant and the time to heal. This is the time to build up and to laugh and to dance. This is the time to sow seeds of health and wholeness. This is the time to embrace and to cherish, the time to look into our brother's eyes and see the vastness of the sea; the time to look on our sister's heart and hear the pulsing rhythm of the universe, to stand in awe before Earth and all the stars.

There is a Buddhist term, *mindfulness*, which quite simply describes the energy to experience the present, to witness deeply everything that is happening in the current moment. Mindfulness is to be aware and alive to what is going on within and without. I hope Earth and All the Stars will engender such an attitude in the minds and hearts of readers. The creation stories, prayers, poems, hymns, songs, and reflections drawn from the great cultures and religions of the world were selected for this purpose. A few are very familiar; many are new. The vedas of antiquity, some as old as three thousand years, have a freshness that transcends time. The truths of God and creation are eternal and they are always, in every age, timely.

My thinking has evolved considerably since the first time I taught a new course in ecology and justice at the Hartford Seminary 1991. I began with just two convictions. First, that Christians had a clear mandate to care for God's creation and that there was plenty to support that responsibility in traditional Hebrew and Christian scripture. Thus there was no need to look anywhere beyond Judeo-Christian tradition to develop a theology of ecology. Second, that the examination of the major issues of ecology (pollution of water, land, air and space; population and poverty; the depletion of natural resources; the interaction of military power and environmental degradation; the relationship between the global economy and the environment; environmental racism), would be enough to engender a heightened awareness of a planet in peril and encourage the students to take corrective action.

And so the course met and students diligently researched their assignments as the weeks rolled on. The topics engaged them and, through lively sharing of insights, we all had our consciousness raised. But I also began to notice a slight, unspoken sense of growing frustration. I asked why that should be. "Yes, we can take action," they said. "We can and we will call our senators and members of congress as issues affecting the environment come up on the federal agenda. We can boycott the products of companies who dump their waste irresponsibly and support those with clean records." They could do all of that and they did. But they wanted more. They wanted to celebrate through prayer and song the wonders of God's creation. They wanted to repent for the ways they and their lifestyles had contributed to the disfiguring of creation. They wanted to offer their concerns for the environment to God. So quite spontaneously, one day, we began singing lines such as "For the beauty of the earth" and "morning has broken, like the first morning." Later, we wrote our own prayers and adapted others. We learned to weave our particular environmental concerns into a litany entitled "God of All Power." We did the same with psalms. We read about the peaceful kingdom (Isaiah 11:6–9), about taking responsibility in the "land of flowing streams" (Deuteronomy 8), Jesus' references to seeds and harvest. We talked about extending the "fruits of the Spirit" (Galatians 5:22–26) to include not only the people of God, but every aspect of God's creation. We fell into a pattern of devoting the last half hour of every class to some sort of worship built upon the environmental issues we had been examining that day. This was an entirely unexpected but nurturing evolution in the course. Thus the first seeds of *Earth and All the Stars* were sown.

As time went on, I collected prayers and readings relating to creation and I continuously searched for more. Visiting a new city or with a few hours to spare, I'd visit the public library. The main public library of Portland, Oregon, was particularly fruitful. I explored university libraries. I combed the sources at the World Council of Churches in Geneva. At Iona, a small island off the west coast of Scotland, I got in touch with my Celtic roots while pursuing my goal. The Celtic Christianity of the second and third centuries speaks with uncanny clarity to those of us poised on the edge of the third

millennium. Missionaries did not eradicate the indigenous religious rites —
so focused on the natural world — that they found in these windswept lands.
Rather, they built Christianity onto the pagan foundations. The result is a
pleasing wedding of traditions. Celtic Christianity thus opens to us a view
of the cosmic sense of God's presence throughout all of creation; in the
land, the rocks, the mountains and hills. God in the waters and in the eye of
the storm, God in and through, under and over, every thing and being in the
universe. It is no accident that Ireland's earliest recorded poem, written one
hundred years before the birth of Christ, begins "I *am* the wind...."

Then I took my first trip to Japan. In Kyoto alone there are some two
thousand Shinto and Buddhist temples or shrines. They are literally everywhere — in residential neighborhoods, on street corners and commercial
areas, in markets, along roadways, and in places of natural beauty. In the
United States and Europe, blaze marks painted on tree trunks and rocks
point the hiker up the mountain trail. In Japan, the hiker follows the path
from shrine to shrine. I got a powerful sense of the holy in Japan. As I walked
along the streets and through the green hills, I sensed the graciousness of the
people as they acknowledged each other — and complete strangers such as
myself — with smiles and bows.

This impression clashed sharply with my expectations of high-tech,
super-power Japan which, along with the United States, is one of the world's
worst despoilers of the environment. There is another Japan that I was priv-
ileged to discover. This is the Japan of high, lush mountains, crashing waterfalls and clear streams; the Japan of cool bamboo forests and luscious tiers
of verdant rice paddies. Here true holiness is to be found. This holiness, felt
walking through the Kurama Temple in Kyoto, convinced me that my sights

had been far too narrow in collecting only Christian sources.

It was a chilly but sunny day during the Golden Week Festival and, with my companions, I had taken a little wooden train up to the foot of Kurama Mountain. We walked through the pretty village of Kurama, over the stream, and through the giant vermilion *torii* where the temple path begins. A Japanese temple is more than buildings; it is woods, gardens, ponds, waterfalls, and streams. It is giant gongs, incense, candles, and prayer boards. It covers anything from a city block to an entire mountain, and may be a mix of Buddhist and Shinto artifacts. As we climbed Kurama Mountain, we passed the shrines, some with incense burners, others with water slowly dripping into cool stone basins. Members of the Kurama school of Buddhism believe that six million years ago, Mao-son, the king of the conqueror of evil and the spirit of the earth, descended upon Mount Kurama from Venus to save the earth. In 770 A.D., a temple was built on Mount Kurama to honor Mao-son — also known as Sonten — and to bear witness to the sacredness of creation.

At the main temple building I came across an explanation of the Sonten trinity in which the spirit of the moon is understood as love, the spirit of the sun as light, and the spirit of the earth as power. Along with it I discovered the "Prayer for Happiness to the Sonten of Kuramayama." With slight adaptations and a different title ("Prayer of Love, Light, and Power"), this beautiful prayer became the first non-Christian selection of my collection. Its few words strengthened my own Christian faith. Its power moved me into a greater sense of awe at the goodness of God's creation. As I continued my walk down the back side of Kurama through the bamboo forest, I knew that I had literally had a mountain-top experience. A door had been opened, and before me lay a treasure trove. I was filled with an insatiable desire to discover the wealth of readings affirming the goodness of creation from other traditions of the world to add to the Christian sources. Through them I had an inkling that my Christianity would continue to deepen and that I might arrive at a more global sense of wonder at what God — the God of a thousand names and faces — is doing to call the people of the earth to honor, cherish, restore, and protect this fragile planet.

A splendid path had been set out for me. I have discovered many treasures in the National Library at the Georges Pompidou Center in Paris. I was drawn to the ancient Hindu vedas, composed sometime between 3000 and 2000 B.C.E., poems of wonder and praise celebrating the gifts of nature and humankind's relationship to the natural world. I studied the *Tao Te Ching*, written some twenty-five hundred years ago by Lao Tzu. We know almost nothing about this poet, yet he expresses in stark simplicity the idea that human beings are to fit into and blend with creation and not the reverse. While these works were not new to me, I read them with a new depth of understanding. I also identified a number of ancient and modern literary treasures from Japan, Korea, the Philippines and especially the Chinese landscape poetry of the T'ang and Sung Dynasties (618 to 960 B.C.E. and 960 to 1127 B.C.E.). T'ang and Sung poets display a range and richness of expression. They were grounded in the belief that knowing the position of the human being in the totality of the universe is the height of wisdom.

Poetry and painting went together in the ancient Chinese world. The painter would create the landscape on the silk screen and then write a few words to express the mood and spirit of the painting. The creation of paintings and poetry were seen as spiritual exercises. Whatever it was that the artist was painting, whether fish, rock, tree, or mountain, the artist, at the moment of painting the subject, was expected to *feel* its nature. If the subject was a tree, the artist *felt* the tree's strength shooting through the branches and down into its roots; if a flower, the artist attempted to *feel* its lightness and grace as its petals unfolded.

One of the underlying principles of *bokugwa* (the name given to this art form) is that it is impossible to express in art what one does not feel. When painting a storm, the artist must feel the rain and crushing wind as it tears trees from their roots and drenches the countryside. To feel the subject of the painting meant getting into the very heart of its nature, to become, as it were, the tree, the rock, the flower. The highest compliment to these artists was — and still is — to say that they paint with their souls; that their brush strokes follow the dictates of their spirit. And it is the same with the poet who writes from the heart of nature, listening attentively to the promptings of her soul.

The contemporary Japanese author Ki no Tsurayuki said, "When we hear the warbling of the mountain thrush in the blossoms or the voice of the frog in the water, we know every living being has a song." It is a song of the ten million sounds of the earth and all the stars. The Christian theologian David Tracy said "there is a new form of spiritual journey, new for Christianity and for all the traditions.…The new search is likely to become that of more and more religious persons. Stay faithful to your own tradition; go more and more deeply into its particularities; defend and clarify its identity. At the same time, wander Ulysses-like, willingly, even eagerly, among other great traditions and ways; try to learn something of their beauty and truth; concentrate on their otherness and difference as the new route to communicality."

Earth and All the Stars is an invitation to "wander Ulysses-like" through the ecological treasures of the world's great religions and cultures; like the Chinese poet/painter, to *feel* Mother Earth beneath your feet and to *feel for* her. So come, Lovers of the Earth, come down to the singing river where our Creator God is beckoning us all to listen to the music of the heavens. Take off your shoes. Feel the rhythm of the universe. Declare a Jubilee for Mother Earth.

Chapter 1

CREATION STORIES
AND REFLECTIONS

In the beginning God created the heavens and the earth.

— Genesis 1:1

WARRIORS OF THE RAINBOW

William Willoya and Vinson Brown

An old Indian woman told the following story to her great grandson:

In their dreams the old ones saw that the Indians would go through a very bad time, that they would lose their spirit, that they would be split up into many parts by the different kinds of religion of the white people. Like them, they would try to find what these strange people call success. But one day the Indians would begin to wake up, the old ones told me. They would see that those white people who chased after personal pleasure left behind the truly important things in life. The Indians would see that their people in the old days were in tune with something far more wonderful; they were in harmony with the Spirit of Life.

And you must realize that this is not all the old ones saw in their dreams. They saw that just when the Indians seemed to be all becoming like the more foolish white people, just when everybody thought they had forgotten about the ancient days, at that time a great light would come from the east. It would come into the hearts of some of the Indians, and they would become like the prairie fire, spreading not only love between all races, but also between the different religions.

This light *you* must find, O son of my son's son, my beloved, and I believe that when you seek for your vision on the mountain top you will be told *how* to find it. For it will be something so big and wonderful that in it all peoples of the world can find shelter. And, in that day all the little circles will come under the one big circle of understanding and unity.

As she stopped talking, the old woman and the boy looked to the east and they saw a great rainbow flaming in the sky where a thunderstorm had passed.

The rainbow is a sign from the Great Spirit who is in all things. It is a sign of the union of all people like one big family. Go to the mountaintop, child of my flesh, and learn to be a Warrior of the Rainbow, for it is only by spreading love and joy to others that hate in this world can be changed to understanding and kindness, and war and destruction shall end.

A copy of the book containing this message was taken by the crew of the Phyllis Cormack *on the first Greenpeace campaign to Amchitka in the Aleutians in September 1971. This legend expressed the spiritual framework for Greenpeace. From it, Greenpeace took the name of the flagship of their fleet, the* Rainbow Warrior, *which was tragically destroyed in an act of sabotage in Auckland, New Zealand on July 10, 1985.*

C*

THE GOLDEN WOMB OF THE SUN

Rig-Veda

In the beginning was the golden womb of the sun,
Only he and nothing else.
He established the earth and the sky.

Even the brightest gods respect his words.
Breath-giver, life-giver,
One half of his shadow is immortality, the other half death.

Mighty ruler,
Lord of the breathing and sleeping world,
King of man and beast.

The snowy mountains declare his glory.
The rivers and the sea declare his glory.
The mountains and the waters are his twin arms.

He made firm the earth and the starry sky,
Earth and the sky-y ether.
He measured the air in the firmament.

Two armies, sky and earth, tremble,
Clash, or stand firm in his will.
The risen sun looks over his shoulder.

Everywhere are the great waters,
Carrying the golden womb of the sun:
From them came light, the breath of the gods.

He looks on the waters,
Powerful and shining;
Pleased with himself, God above all other gods.

God of the earth,
     protect us;
God of the sky,
     protect us;
God of the great and shining waters,
     protect us.

God above all other gods,
God of the Golden sun, God of all,
we shall worship you.

The creation story "The Golden Womb of the Sun" comes from the most ancient of Hinduism's revealed scriptures, the Rig-Veda, probably composed sometime between 3000 and 2000 B.C.E. The Rig-Veda is the oldest document of the world's living religions and is made up of animistic songs and prayers personifying nature and attributing divine personalities to its forces.

☪

THE CREATION

James Weldon Johnson

And God stepped out in space
And he looked around and said:
I'm lonely —
I'll make me a world.

And far as the eye of God could see
Darkness covered everything,
Blacker than a hundred midnights
Down in a cypress swamp.

Then God smiled,
And the light broke,
And the darkness rolled up on one side,
And the light stood shining on the other,
And God said: That's good!

Then God reached out and took the light in His hands,
And God rolled the light around in His hands
Until He made the sun;
And He set that sun a-blazing in the heavens.
And the light that was left from making the sun
God gathered it up in a shining ball

And flung it against the darkness,
Spangling the night with the moon and stars.
Then down between
The darkness and the light
He hurled the world:
And God said: That's good!

Then God himself stepped down —
And the Sun was on His right hand,
And the moon was on His left;
The stars were clustered about His head,
And Earth was under His feet.
And God walked, and where He trod
His footsteps hollowed the valleys out
And bulged the mountains up.

Then He stopped and looked and saw
That Earth was hot and barren.
So God stepped over the edge of the world
And He spat out the seven seas —
He batted His eyes, and the lightnings flashed —
He clapped His hands, and the thunders rolled —
And the waters above Earth came down,
The cooling waters came down.

Then the green grass sprouted,
And the little red flowers blossomed,

The pine tree pointed his finger to the sky,
And the oak spread out his arms,
The lakes cuddled down in the hollows of the ground,
And the rivers ran down to the sea;
And God smiled again.
And the rainbow appeared,
And curled itself around His shoulder.

Then God raised His arm and He waved His hand
Over the sea and over the land,
And He said: Bring forth! Bring forth!
And quicker than God could drop His hand,
Fishes and fowls,
And beasts and birds
Swam the rivers and the seas,
Roamed the forests and the woods,
And split the air with their wings,
And God said: That's good!

Then God walked around,
And God looked around
On all that He had made.
He looked at His sun,
And He looked at His moon,
And He looked at His little stars;
He looked on His world

With all its living things,
And God said: I'm lonely still.

Then God sat down —
On the side of a hill where He could think;
By a deep, wide river He sat down;
With His head in His hands,
God thought and thought,
Till He thought: I'll make me a man!

Up from the bed of the river
God scooped the clay;
And by the bank of the river
He kneeled Him down;
And there the great God Almighty
Who lit the sun and fixed it in the sky,
Who flung the stars to the most far corner of the night,
Who rounded Earth in the middle of His hand;
This Great God,
Like a mammy bending over her baby,
Kneeled down in the dust
Toiling over a lump of clay
Till He shaped it in His own image.
Then into it He blew the breath of life,
And man became a living soul.
Amen. Amen.

Twentieth-century African American poet, diplomat, and anthologist of black culture James Weldon Johnson (1871–1938) offers an interpretation of the biblical creation narrative. "The Creation" is a sermon in verse, taken from Johnson's best-known work, God's Trombones, *published in 1927.*

☾*

CREATION STORY: A RETELLING

Moyra Caldecott

"In the beginning was the Word, and the Word was with God,
and the Word was God."   — *John* 1:1

Outside Time the Consciousness of God exists.
In that Consciousness
is a thought
of such intensity that within it
all and everything
conceivable and inconceivable,
imaginable and unimaginable,
possible and impossible
is contained.
That thought is uttered
and from the vibrations of that sound,

from the resonance of that Word,
from what the scientists call
"The Big Bang,"
the multitudinous forms of being are spreading
in ever increasing circles.

The vast universe of whirling forms takes shape.
World after world swings through space,
each to each held
by an inner and invisible force,
the whole
a balance of attraction and repulsion.
Within these worlds
light and dark interact.
Eons pass.
Liquid fire cools to rock,
scalding steam to rain.
More than a thousand million years pass.
More than a thousand million times
the burning orb of the sun rises and sets
over the desolate landscapes of our earth —
its powerful cosmic rays ever active, ever potent.

Cautiously the first life forms emerge —
infinitesimal cells divide, join up with others,
subdivide, rejoin.
The liquid oceans seethe with life.

Beings with or without calcareous shells
live and die by their billions
trilobites
graptolites
brachiopods
drifting through the waters for three hundred million years
to lie at last on the ancient sea bed,
their minute bodies
forming the fossiliferous rock
we walk so casually upon today,
while the shell of the ammonite
that pumped through the primal ocean
so vigorously in search of food
has been replaced molecule by molecule by crystal
and lies now, bejeweled, in our museums,
curled, whorled, and spiraled.

Some life-forms collect in rock pools,
breathe air,
grow and change.
The first fish struggle on to land
exchanging fins for limbs.
Corals and sponges build their sturdy tenements
and learn communal living in the oceans.

On land, cold-blooded reptiles sun themselves singly
upon the rocks,

mosses and horsetail plants as tall as forest trees
flourish in the marshlands.
Three hundred and fifty million years ago
the coal beds formed as these marshland forests died.
Another two hundred million years
and the dinosaurs tread hot sand
leaving their giant footsteps, fossilized.
Where have they gone, these ancient fearsome beasts?
They with the tiny ammonites and belemnites are now extinct.
Do we still carry them in our blood?

Time moves on.
Small warm-blooded mammals take their place
among the cycads, gingkoes, ferns, and conifers.
Birds sing
and the first flowering plants put out their finery.
Another sixty million years go by
and we rise to our feet,
lift our eyes to the firmament
and begin to name names
and recognize our God.
Still with us
is the first impetus of the Word.

Our being is the expression of God's Thought.
We contain the love of God and God contains us

and as we unfold on earth
through shell-creature,
fish-form,
reptile,
bird,
and mammal —
through icthyosaurs
plesiosaurs
dinosaurs
and ape —
we are learning
step by step
what that containment means.

The circles are still widening —
still evolving the mighty concept —
the magnificent Idea.
Six days,
Seven...
a million years,
a thousand million...
the count is nothing,
the Being — All.
Praise be to our great God
and the Word that resonates
in our hearts still.

May we not separate ourselves in arrogance
from the Great Work
for we know the sound of the Word
but not its full meaning.

Usually Christians look to the Book of Genesis for a biblical account of creation, yet Moyra Caldecott has used the opening verse of Saint John's Gospel to great effect in inviting us to marvel, in the present tense, at the wonder of creation and the immensity of time it is taking for the "Great Work" to come into being. This story was first used in Coventry Cathedral in England for a Creation Festival liturgy.

☪*

PRAISE BELONGS TO GOD

Selected Readings on Creation from the Koran Interpreted

Praise belongs to God
who created the heavens and the earth
and appointed the shadows and light. . . .
It is God who created you out of clay.
He is God in the heavens and the earth.

God subjected the sun and the moon,
each one running to a term stated.

It is the Holy One who stretched out the earth
and stretched therein
firm mountains and rivers,
and every fruit.

God is He that looses the winds
that stir up the dust...
God created you of dust
then a sperm-drop.
Then He made you pairs.

Not equal are the two seas;
this one is gentle, grateful to taste,
delicious to drink,
and that is salt, bitter to the tongue.
Yet both you eat.

The cattle —
God created them for you;
in them is warmth, and uses various,
and of them you eat.
There is beauty in them for you,
when you bring them home to rest
and when you drive them forth abroad to pasture.
They bear your loads
unto a land that you would never reach.

Surely your God is All-clement, All-compassionate,
for He created horses, and mules and asses for you to ride.

Praise belongs to God,
Originator of the heavens and earth,
who appointed the angels to be messengers
having wings, two, three, and four,
increasing creation as he wills.

O people, remember God's blessing upon you;
is there any creator, apart from God,
who provides for you out of heaven and earth?
God's promise is true.

The Koran is the book of Islam, which is believed to have been revealed to the prophet Mohammed (ca. 570–629) through the mediation of the archangel Gabriel. It embodies the basic principles of Islamic law. The Koran is second only to the Bible in its influence on Western civilization. Muslims believe that there is only one Koran, written in Arabic, which cannot be translated. Any translations into other languages, such as this one, are considered interpretations. Arthur John Arberry's interpretation, first published in 1955, is still recognized as one of the most accurate and prosaic.

☪*

OTOKAHEKAGAPI

First Beginnings, a Lakota Creation Story

Thomas E. Simms and Ben Black Bear Jr.

Before any other thing Inyan (the Rock) was. And his spirit was Wakan Tanka (the Great Holy God). Before the four times Inyan was. Han (Darkness) was then, but she was not a thing. She was only the black darkness. Inyan possessed all powers then and the powers were in his blood, and his blood was blue. Inyan grew lonely and longed for an other. Inyan knew that there could be none other unless he took from himself. To take from himself he would have to let his blood flow from him, and he knew that as his blood would leave him, so would his powers.

So Inyan said *"Nunwe!"* (So be it!) and this was the first sound. Then Inyan took from himself and let himself flow outward around himself in the form of a great sphere. And Inyan named the sphere Maka (Earth). Inyan opened all his veins and his blood left him, and Inyan saw that his powers went from him in the blood and formed the edge of Maka. And where the edge of Maka was there was no beyond. There was only the darkness of Han.

Inyan shrank and grew hard, but he still sought to control his powers. His blood became the waters but the powers flowed outward from the waters and formed around Maka as the spirit. And the powers became Skan (the Sky). Skan is the powers around Maka, and Skan is Nagi Tanka (the Great Spirit).

Maka, the Earth, pouted because she had not been made a separate thing and because the powers had left her with Skan. Maka was conscious and saw herself, and she was naked and cold. All around her was the cold darkness of Han. Maka nagged Inyan to banish Han. She demanded to be made separate. But Inyan said that he was helpless to placate her, for his powers had left him and had become Skan.

At last Inyan and Maka agreed to petition Skan to solve their desires. So Skan heard the complaint of Maka and the plea of Inyan. And he decreed that he would be the judge of their dispute — he would be the great judge. Skan commanded that Maka must remain united with Inyan as she was made, but to please her he would banish Han. So Skan banished Han to the outer regions, and made Anp (Light), but Anp was not a thing, he was only the red of light. And this was the first light, but there was no heat or shadow.

Skan made manifest a great shining thing, round like Maka, the world, and he named this Wi (Sun). Skan commanded Wi to shine and to give heat, and to make a shadow for all that was. And Wi did as he was commanded, and all the world was hot except where there was shadow.

Then Maka had no relief from the heat of Wi and she pouted. She begged Skan to return Han to her and Skan heard the complaint of Maka. So Skan commanded Han to return, and he decreed that Han should be with Maka for a space, and then Anp would be with Maka for a space, and thus each would follow after the other so that Maka would have relief from the heat of Wi. Then Skan commanded that Wi should go before Anp to the regions beyond the world, but that Anp would be the forerunner of Wi when he returned to the world. They did as commanded, so there was light and heat upon the world. The light time Skan named Anp-etu (Day Light), and the dark time he named Han-yetu (Dark Night) and they followed after one another and Maka was pleased.

Thus came into being the four superior mysteries that are the world, and are of the world and they are named Wakan Kin (the Holy Mysteries). And they are named Wakan Ankantu (Great Holy Mysteries). These mysteries are sacred and immortal: Wikan (Sun Immortal), Tokan (Blue Sky Immortal), Makakan (Earth Immortal) and Inyankan (Rock Immortal). And they counseled together with Skan as the judge, and Skan decreed that they would be recognized and would rank in order of their importance: Wi would rank first, and his color would be red. Skan himself would rank second, and his color would be blue. Maka is third, and her color would be green. And Inyan fourth, and his color would be yellow. United they would all be the colors as like a rainbow, and they would be one thing: the Superior Mystery, the Great Spirit. But the spirit of all is Wakan Tanka, the Great Mystery, the Great Holy God, that not even they can understand.

Who am I? Where did I come from? How was the world created at the beginning of time? These identity questions are basic to all peoples, cultures, and religious traditions. Answers to them are attempts to find our historical place in the cosmos. "Otokahekagapi" is a Lakota creation story, an account of the beginnings of the western band of Plains people also known as the Sioux.

☪*

WELL I'LL BE

A Filipino Creation Story

Author Unknown

In the beginning the Great Spirit created the Universe. Now the universe was dark. So the Great Spirit said, "Let there be light." And behold, light appeared.

Then the Great Spirit said, "Let the heavens be." And behold, the heavens blossomed into galaxies filled with stars, planets, and moons.

The Great Spirit said, "Let the plants be." And behold, the Earth began to green with mosses, ferns, vines, trees, flowers, and grasses.

Then the Great Spirit said, "Let the animals be." And behold, countless creatures emerged to crawl, walk, fly, and swim over the land, sea, and sky.

All creatures needed and helped each other to stay alive. The sun gave its life to the plants; the plants gave their lives to the animals; the animals gave their lives to the worms; the worms gave their lives to the soil; and the soil gave its life to the plants.

The sun's heat formed clouds that watered the rainforest; the forest's canopy caught the lashing rain and dropped it gently into streams and rivers that continually watered the lowlands.

The rivers passed through the mangrove forests bringing water and soil for the trees. The swamp, in turn, purified the muddy rivers for the coastal reefs, which need crystal-clear water to survive.

Soon all creatures on earth began to sing:

"This earth spun of soil and sun,
Water and air for all to share,
Lives or dies by the work and play
Of every creature, every day."

Then Great Spirit danced to the song of her creation. "Well I'll be!" She exclaimed, "This is wonderful."

The suddenly the first humans appeared, for the Great Spirit had accidentally created creatures in her own image when she said, "Well I'll be." And today, human beings feel most alive when they dance with the song of the earth and sky.

"Well I'll Be," a Filipino creation story, was identified by Matthew Fox when he was leading a creation spirituality workshop in the Philippines. A significant feature of this account is that God, the Great Spirit who created the universe, is portrayed as feminine.

C*

BEFORE GOD CREATED THE WORLD

A Sikh Creation Narrative

Japji Sahib and Rag Gaur Bairagan

Before God created the world there was no earth nor sky, nor sun or human; neither Brahma nor Vishnu. The cycle of birth and death, pleasure and pain, and the sacred scriptures were all nonexistent. No creatures, no humans, nothing at all existed. God alone existed in this *Akhand Smadhi* (unbroken trance) until he decided to create our world. God, the creator, brought all the worlds and the underworlds into existence through the Divine Word. Guru Nānak said, "God spoke once and there was creation."

For millions and millions of countless years was spread darkness when existed neither earth nor human but only the Limitless Divine Ordinance. Then existed neither day nor light nor sun nor moon. The Creator into unbroken trance was absorbed. Then were not Brahma, Vishnu, or Shiva, none other than the sole God was visible. Neither existed then female or male or caste or birth. None suffering or joy received. Then were not instituted recitation of scripture or keeping of vows, fasts, or worship offerings. Then, creating continents, spheres and nether worlds, the hidden God made himself manifest.

As their creator, the natural beauty that exists and can be found in all living things whether animals, birds, fish, belongs to God and God alone is their ruler. Without God's order, nothing exists, changes, or develops.

Having brought the world into being, God sustains, nourishes, and protects it. Nothing is overlooked. Even creatures in rocks and stones are well
provided for. Birds who fly thousands of miles away leaving their young ones
behind know that they will be sustained and taught to fend for themselves by
God. The creatures of nature lead their lives under God's command and with
God's grace. Guru Nānak applauds their closeness to God and his creation
in this hymn:

> If I were a doe living in the forest, eating grass and leaves,
>> with God's grace I would find God.
> If I were a cuckoo living in the mango tree,
>> contemplating and singing,
>> God would reveal divine mercy.
> If I were a female snake, dwelling in the ground,
>> God's word would be in my being,
>> my dread would vanish.
> Eternal God is found,
>> light meets light.

*Sikhs hold that the universe is composed of five elements: air, water, earth, fire, and space.
Water is the father, Earth the mother. God, who brought everything into being, is a personal
God who continues to nourish and sustain every aspect of creation.*

C*

ENTERING THE TWENTY-FIRST CENTURY

Thich Nhat Hanh

It is important that the young people [who have suffered so much from the wars and atrocities of this century] and the generation responsible for the wars begin anew, and together create a path of mindfulness so that our children in the next century can avoid repeating the same mistakes.

The flower of tolerance to see and appreciate cultural diversity is one flower we can cultivate for the children of the twenty-first century. Another flower is the truth of suffering — there has been so much unnecessary suffering in our century. If we are willing to work together and learn together, we can all benefit from the mistakes of our time, and, seeing with the eyes of compassion and understanding, we can offer the next century a beautiful garden and a clear path.

Take the hand of your child and invite her to go out and sit with you on the grass. The two of you may want to contemplate the green grass, the little flowers that grow among the grasses, and the sky. Breathing and smiling together — this is peace education. If we know how to appreciate these beautiful things, we will not have to search for anything else. Peace is available in every moment, in every breath, in every step.

Coming from the beautiful but war-wracked country of Vietnam, Thich Nhat Hanh is passionate about our shared responsibility for building world peace and a healthy planet where the forces of war, greed, pride of nations, consumerism, and selfishness are overcome by universal love, justice, dignity, and respect for every being in creation.

☾*

THE HOLY ONE HAS MADE ALL THINGS

Sirach 43

The pride of the higher realms is the clear vault of the sky, as glorious to behold as the sight of the heavens. The sun, when it appears, proclaims as it rises what a marvelous instrument it is, the work of the Most High. At noon it parches the land, and who can withstand its burning heat. It breathes out fiery vapors. Great is the God who made it.

It is the moon that marks the changing seasons, governing the times, their everlasting sign. From the moon comes the sign of festal days, a light that wanes when it completes its course. The new moon renews itself. How marvelous it is in this change, a beacon to the hosts on high, shining in the vault of the heavens.

The glory of the stars is the beauty of heaven, a glittering array in the heights of Heaven. On the orders of the Holy One they stand in their appointed places; they never relax in their watches.

Look at the rainbow, and praise God who made it; it is exceedingly beautiful in its brightness. It encircles the sky with its glorious arc; the hands of the Most High have stretched it out.

The Holy One sends the driving snow and speeds the lightning. God's storehouses are opened and the clouds fly out like birds. In majesty God gives the clouds their strength and the hailstones are broken in pieces. God's voice, like a thunder clap, rebukes the earth. When the Holy One appears, the mountains shake. At God's will the south wind blows; so do the storms from the north and the whirlwinds.

The Holy One scatters the snow like birds flying down and its descent is like locusts alighting. The eye is dazzled by the beauty of its whiteness and the mind is amazed as it falls. God pours frost over the earth like salt and icicles form like pointed thorns. The cold north wind blows and ice freezes on the water. It settles on every pool of water and the water puts it on like a breastplate.

God consumes the mountains and burns up the wilderness. God withers the tender grass like fire. A mist quickly heals all things; the falling dew gives refreshment from the heat.

By divine plan the Most High stilled the deep and planted islands in it. In it are strange and marvelous creatures, all kinds of living things, and the huge whales of the sea.

Because of the great God of all creation all things hold together. Awesome is the Holy One and very great. Marvelous is God's power who has made all things.

The book of Sirach is included in the Apocrypha, which consists of the Biblical books received by the early church as part of the Greek version of the Old Testament, but not included in the Hebrew Bible. This selection presents a sweeping, poetic, compelling image of the all-powerful God who created the sun, moon, stars, fire, water, lightning, clouds as well as all manner of plants, animals, fish, and people. The Great God who created it all continues to uphold and sustain the universe.

☾*

SILENCE

Peter Gold

The occasional bleat of a sheep,
    bang of a bell,
    a snatch of song by a villager harvesting her field,
    are all that one can hear.

Otherwise, silence.

Silence, like an infinity view down the spreading valley.
Silence, like the clouds gathering momentarily above it.
Silence, like the sandy gullies that turn into boiling torrents
      when the heavy rains eventually come.
Silence, like the narrow lane curling around one mountain's base
      then the next.
Silence, like the wildflowers subtly swaying
      to the touch of an unseen breeze.
Silence, golden like the sun now beginning to flood the landscape
      with warmth, bringing life wherever it goes.
Silence, in solitude, brings one great solace,
      atop the altar of the earth.

The ancients of Asia often believed that the gods descended to earth from mountaintops. Even modern poets find power and a sense of holiness in the high and quiet places "atop the altar of the earth."

☪*

TOWARD THE BOSOM OF THE NEWLY RISING SUN

Tujin Pak

Behold the sun. Behold the sun blaze fire as it rises.
Let us walk on the fresh fragrant grass when the sun
rises over the hill. Let us take the dazzling path at dawn
toward the sun.

Be gone, Darkness. Be gone, Darkness that moans
like a beast. Be gone, like beasts, herding onto the cliff.
Onto the cliff, sunlight loaded on your back.

Behold those mountain flowers giving a pungent smell.
Behold those green leaves of trees fluttering as if they dance.
Listen to the melodies of birds, to the song of the waters that
meander through the valleys. The sound that the whole
mountain makes as it wakes again to receive the light.

The grass sound the grass makes on its leaves.
The leaf sound the trees make on their leaves.
The fish sound the minnow-like silver fish make.
As they mill around in schools in the clear water.
The stone sound the stones make as they are tossed down.

The measuring worms on the branches and
    the slugs on the bottom.
Cheered, I shout "yahoy ho," baptized in the sun.

Low and faint but withering in unison
rings the songbird of all things green in the mountain.
Of all living things in the mountain.

Mountain, green mountain with leaves of trees fluttering.

When the sun leaps and radiates
My ears open at your fresh sounds;

My eyes brighten at your fresh light.
Blood circulates afresh.

The whole body tingles as if to soar into the air.
I feel light as a bird,
As I walk onto the green morning road,
Walk toward the bosom of the newly rising sun.

The Korean poet, Tujin Pak (b. 1916), has always taken his themes from the physical world — mountains, trees, the sea, the sun. Read this poem outside in a place of natural beauty when you greet the new day.

☾*

LEARN FROM THE PINE

Bashō

Learn about pines from the pine, and about bamboo from the bamboo.

Make the universe your companion, always bearing in mind the true nature of things — mountains and rivers, trees and grasses, and humanity — and enjoy the falling blossoms and the scattering leaves.

It is this poetic spirit that leads one to follow nature and become a friend with things of the seasons. For a person who has the spirit, everything she sees becomes a flower, and everything he imagines turns into the moon.

Every form of insentient existence — plants, stones, or utensils — has its individual feelings similar to those of people. When we observe calmly, we discover that all things have their fulfillment.

Bashō (1644–1694), Japan's most famous poet, kept travel journals while on pilgrimage. Many have become classics of Japanese literature. "Learn from the Pine" provides us with a well-phrased Zen way of meditating on nature.

C*

I AM THE SUNRISE

Compiled by Matthew Fox

I am the sunrise that brightens up the sky in the early morning.

I am the rays of the sun that give radiance to every creature during the
sunrise at Manila Bay.

I am the beam of the waterfalls.

I am the fire that kindles the stars, and the stars in your eyes.

I am the precious jewel out of the bowels of the earth, gifted with
beauty to bring radiance to all creatures.

I am the sound that penetrates the hearts of all creatures.

I am the water from the primeval ocean, where you slept in your mother's
womb.

I am the white sand kissed by the bubbling waves of the blue seas.

I am the restless waves slapping the seashore of the industrialized world.

I am the running water that gives joy to dying creatures.

I am the spring that quenches the thirst of the displaced animals.

I am the wind that soothes the feelings of every tree, meadow, and race.

I am the breeze that caresses you.

I am the fresh smell of the rice fields.

I am the earth that shaped you from tiny dust.

I am the trunk of a talisay tree standing amidst the polluted and
overpopulated urban areas.

I am the tall and stately coconut trees that line the shores.

I am the sturdy bamboo that sways unbroken by strong winds,

and dances to the rhythm of the gentle breeze.
I am the giant eagle that flies searching for tall trees.
I am the forest cool with sun's early morning rays.
I am the weaver of your stories and dreams that clothe the universe!

I am the mighty wind that howls and growls.
I am the wind of land and sea.
I am the soft breeze that soothes your suffering.
I am the soft glow of the moon in a clear starry night.
I am the power of the growing trees.
I am the power that propels your growth.
I am the bud breaking into blossoms.
I am the clear streams where fish abound for the sustenance of life.

I am the sweat of an oppressed people.
I am the smile on the lip of a fallen comrade.
I am the tears of a mother in pain.
I am the sea that cleanses and purifies.
I am the sea that guards and challenges and never sleeps.
I am the coconut tree sucking up the undrinkable salt water and
    offering it as healing.
I am deep brown eyes gently and quickly connecting all beings.
I am the rainbow of your life.
I am the color of the rainbow that gives hope.
I am the laughter of a newborn child and I am the weeping of a
    battered child.

I am the breath that gives life to all creation.

I am the song that endlessly rocks the cradle of the universe.
I am the dance that turns the feet of the cosmos.
I am the silence that stills the earth, the sea, and sky and all that lives.
I am the all in all.
I am the dance of the dragonfly in the ricefield.
I am the great ball of fire in the core of Mother Earth whose
    rage trembles the mountains and hills.
I am the riches of the earth.
I am the music in every song.
I am the stillness of the raging storm.
I am the empty space that offers all possibilities.
I am the source of breath that is breathed by all.
I am the sound of silence in the deepest silence.
I am the all in all.

I am empty.
I am the dry ground waiting for the rain.
I am the flowing peace.
I am the milky white flower of the sampaguita whose fragrance
    permeates the air.
I am the gentle ripple of the clear stream winding through the forest.
I am the gracefully rushing wind.
I am the bamboo tree.

I am the unseen earthworm burrowing under Mother Earth.

I am the crooning lullaby that rocks the baby to sleep.

I am the forlorn tree resisting extinction.

I am the vision that inspires people to dream.

I am the Filipino soul struggling to be free.

I am the tears of children orphaned by war.

I am the loneliness of men and women who've lost their partners in
    senseless killings.

I am the smoke that rises from dunghills.

I am the flying dust and broken stones from the quarry.

I am the decaying leaves adding my life force to the new plants of spring.

I am the gentle breeze and raging winds that soothe the effects
    of global warming.

I am the heart that longs for endless joy and peace.

I am the starry night that awakens awe in simple hearts.

I am the ocean that brings you the sense of expansiveness.

I am the laughter of little children in tune with gurgling streams.

I am the thunderous blow of the erupting volcano.

I am the void that runs deep and eats the human heart.

I am the overflowing compassion that will fill that void.

I am the plant that has given my beautiful flower back to the earth.

I am the pollen that powders the earth.

I am the plant that struggles to live out of dryness.

I am the rain that waters creation.

I am the shepherd that patiently watches the flock.

I am the food that fills the empty stomach.

I am the eye that sees, the ear that listens to the music of the spheres.

I am the heart that wanders through the wilderness.

I am the ting of the carpenter's hammer.

I am the fisherman setting out into the dark early morning.

I am the moon and stars that guide the fisherfolk home.

I am the ox plowing the field, a faithful friend to the poor farmer.

I am the stream that flows to water the rice fields

I am the mountains, home of the Lumads and the lonely
    dwelling place of the dying rain forest.

I am the Earth.

I am the atom that composes the universe.

I am you, I am he, I am she. ... I am everything that is.

I am. ...

I am the universe, I am the earth.

I am the creatures, powerful and weak.

I am the melody dancing with the wind.

I am the spring that quenches the thirst of weary travelers.

I am the wind that blows upon the earth.

I am the wave that laps the ocean shore.

I am the rays of sun.

I am the bud bursting into fragrance.

I am the choral harmony of chirping cicadas that fill the stillness of the
   night.

I am the trees reaching out to touch the sky.

I am the radiance in the midst of darkness.

I am the beauty walking around the ruins.

I am the power unlocking secrets of the universe.

I am the sparrow singing our victories.

I am what I am — the Holy God of the universe
   who is of all, in all, under all, over all, all.

*"I Am the Sunrise" is the fruit of a creation-reflection spirituality workshop led by
Matthew Fox at Davao, in the Philippines. According to Fox, "one of the exercises we shared
at the workshop was to create together an 'I Am' poem, a poem of the Cosmic Christ in the
Philippines. All of the people were poets that day."*

C*

HEAVEN AND EARTH ABIDE

Selected Readings from Tao Te Ching

Lao Tzu

     Heaven and earth abide.
     By not living for themselves,
          they live forever.

     True goodness is like water.
     Water gives life to ten thousand things
          but does not compete with them.

     Keep to simplicity,
     Grasp the primal,
     Reduce the self,
          and curb desire.

     Twist and get whole.
     Bend and get straight.
     Be empty and get filled.
     Be worn and get renewed.
     Have little; get much.

     The universe has four greats:
     Humanity,

Earth,
Heaven, and the
Tao.
Humanity follows the earth,
Earth follows heaven,
Heaven follows the *Tao,*
The *Tao* follows itself.

The world is a sacred vessel
Not to be acted upon.
Whoever acts upon it
destroys it.
Whoever grasps it
loses it.

Hold to the great *Tao*
and all beneath heaven will follow.

When the Tao is lost,
there is no virtue.
When virtue is lost,
there is no humanness.
When humanness is lost,
there is no morality.
When morality is lost,
there is only ceremony
and the beginning of confusion and folly.

Therefore, the wise person holds to:
The solid,
            rather than the shell;
The fruit rather than the blossom.
S/he avoids the outward,
            and holds to the inward.

The bright way looks dark.
The forward way looks behind.
The smooth way looks rough.
High virtue looks low.

Beneath heaven,
The more laws and prohibitions there are,
            the poorer the people become.
The sharper the country's weapons,
            the greater its confusion.
The cleverer the people become,
            the more deceit takes place.

 A journey of a thousand miles
            starts where your feet are right now.

 When people do not fear force,
            greater force is on the way.

❦ Nothing beneath heaven
is softer and weaker than water.
The weak overcomes the strong,
the soft overcomes the hard.

❦ The more s/he gives,
the more s/he receives.
The way of Heaven is to benefit
but not to harm.
They way of the sage is
to work in concert with heaven.

Tao Te Ching (meaning "the way"), the twenty-five-hundred-year-old treasury of wisdom that originated in China, has maintained its appeal throughout all ages and cultures. In very simple and direct terms it speaks eternal truths to those who seek The Way in all its fullness. The core teaching of Tao Te Ching is that there is an all-suffusing spiritual harmony running throughout creation, an orderly interaction of all life and that the goal of each human being is to put one's self in accord with Tao and thus live in peace and harmony in the world.

☾*

GOD OF THE EARTH, OUR MOTHER, MAKE A WIDE WORLD FOR US

Atharva-Veda

Truth, eternal order, that is great and stern,
    holiness, austerity, prayer, and ritual —
    these uphold the Earth.
May you, queen of what has been and will be,
    make a wide world for us.

Earth which has many heights and slopes and
    unconfined plain that binds everything together,
Earth that bears plants with healing powers,
    may you spread wide for us and thrive.

Earth, in which lie the sea, the rivers, and other waters,
    in which food and cornfields have come to be,
In which live all that breathes and that moves,
    may you confer on us the finest of your yield.

Guardian of the four quarters, in whom
    food and cornfields have come to be,
who bears in many forms the breathing and moving life,
    may you give us cattle and crops.

Earth, in which people of old before us
　　performed their varied works,
Where good overwhelms evil,
Earth, the home of all living things —
　　may you give us magnificent grace.

All sustaining, treasure-bearing, firm foundation,
　　home of all moving life,
Earth bears the sacred universal fire.
May you, God Almighty, protect its wealth.

Earth, whom the celestial guardians protect forever without erring,
　　may you, God of the Earth, pour on us your sweet blessings
　　and endow us with joy.

Earth, which at first was in the water of the ocean;
　　Earth whose spirit is in the eternal Heaven,
　　wrapped in truth immortal,
May you give us wisdom.

Earth, in which the waters, common to all,
　　moving on all sides, flowing unfailing, day and night;
May you pour on us milk of many streams,
　　like a mother to her child,
　　and endow us with constancy.

Pleasant be your hills, O Earth,
>   your snow-clad mountains and your woods!
Oh Earth — brown, black, red, and multi-colored —
>   the firm Earth protected by God,
>   on this Earth may we stand, unvanquished, unslain, unharmed.

Set us, O Earth, amidst what is your center and your navel,
>   and the life-giving forces that emanate from you.
Purify us from all sides.
Earth, you are our mother, we your children:
>   Give us rain in due season and fill us with your plenty.

The evil ones who threaten the Earth
>   with malevolent thoughts and weapons of destruction,
Overwhelm them, O God of the Earth, as you have done before.

Born of you and on you move every living creature;
>   you bear them all — the two legged and four legged.
Yours, O Earth, are all the races of humanity
>   on whom the sun rises and spreads with its rays of light immortal.
In concert, may all creatures pour out unending thanksgivings.

Mother of all plants,
>   firm Earth upheld by eternal law,
May you be ever beneficent and gracious to us,

as we tread upon your lands.
A vast abode you are, and mighty,
      strong is your speed, your moving and your shaking.
You, all powerful God, protect us without ceasing.
May you, O Earth, make us shine forth
      with the brightness of your radiance.

A fire lies deep within the Earth.
      It is in plants and waters and stone.
There is a fire deep within the people,
      a fire in the kilns and a fire in horses.
This is the same fire that burns in the heavens;
      all fire belongs to this Fire Divine.

People of Earth kindle this fire and bear their oblations.
May Earth, clad in her fiery mantle, fire us
      and light our ways.

The fragrance that rises from you, O Earth
      is carried in plants and in the waters.
God of the Earth, protect us with your sweetness and grace.

Rock, soil, stone, and dust by which
      Earth is held together and bound firm;
To you, O God of the Earth, we offer our devotion.

Rising or sitting, standing or walking,
    may we, neither with our right foot or our left,
    ever totter on the earth.

Earth, purifier, patient Earth,
    bearer of power, and plenty.
    sharer of food and molten butter;
May we grow strong through your spiritual might.

May those that are of the eastern regions,
    and the northern and the southern and the western,
    be gentle as they walk upon the Earth.
Protect us from stumbling while we walk upon your world.
As you guide our steps, keep us from being pushed as from the
    West or from the East, or from the North or from the South.
Keep us on the straight path so that we may not wander astray.

As long as we look on you from around, O Earth,
    with the sun as friend,
So long as year follows year,
    may our vision not fail.
When we are lying down, O Earth,
    protect us and all who sleep.

Whatever I dig from you, O Earth,
    may your mantle grow back again quickly.
O Earth, purifier, may we never injure you.

May your summer, O Earth, and your rains,
 your autumn, your dewy months, your winters, and your spring,
May these seasons, Earth, that make the year,
 and day and night
 pour their abundance upon us.

Earth in which are cities, the works of God
 and fields where people are variously employed;
Earth that bears all things in her womb,
 may you, O Lord of Life, make us graceful from every side.

The people of the Earth speak a multitude of tongues,
 they have a variety of religious rites,
 according to their places of abode,
Pour upon us all your treasure in a thousand streams,
 like a cow full of milk that never fails.

The snake and the scorpion with the sharp sting that,
 overpowered by the cold season, lie bewildered in the caves,
The worm and each thing that comes to life, O Earth,
 and moves about with the coming on of rains,
 may these, creeping things, never creep near us.

Your many pathways for folk to travel on,
 the roads for chariots, and for wagons to pass through,
On which walk together both the good and the evil,

may no dangers overcome us, and may thieves and foes be driven
   far from us.

Your forest animals and wild beasts of the woods —
      lions, tigers, man-eaters that prowl about,
The hyena, the wolf, and the bear,
      keep these, O God of the Earth, far away from us.

Earth in which the winged birds fly together —
      swans, eagles, and other birds of various kinds,
      on which the wind blows strong, raising the dust, bending trees,
Earth in which night and day — the black and the bright in union —
      are settled, Earth, which is covered over by rain —
May you, God of all the Earth,
      establish your peace in every home.

In villages, in the forest and in the assemblies on the earth,
      in congregations and in councils, may we speak of
      you, God of Earth, in reverent terms.

As a horse scatters dust, so did Earth, since she was born,
      scatter the people who dwelt on the land,
      and she joyously sped on, the world's protector,
      supporter of forest trees and plants.
Peaceful, sweet-smelling, gracious, filled with milk,
      and bearing nectar,

May the God of the Earth give to us the milk of her blessing.
Bearers of your bounty may our lives be lives of unceasing thanksgivings
    for all the blessings of the Earth.
Earth, our mother, set us on the paths of peace in full
    accord with Heaven.
Holy God, Wise One Immortal, forever keep your Earth in grace and
    splendor.

"God of the Earth, Our Mother, Make a Wide World for Us" comes from the latest of the four Hindu vedas (sacred books of knowledge). It is a beautiful, comprehensive prayer of petition to God rich in feminine imagery, concluding in the final stanza, "May the God of the Earth give us the milk of her blessing"; and "Earth, our mother, set us on the paths of peace in full accord with Heaven."

C*

ANY FOOL CAN DESTROY TREES

John Muir

The axe and saw are insanely busy, chips are flying thick as snowflakes, and every summer thousands of acres of priceless forests, with their under-brush, soil, springs, climate, scenery, and religion, are vanishing away in clouds of smoke.

Any fool can destroy trees. They cannot run away; and if they could, they would still be destroyed — chased and hunted down as long as fun or a dollar could be got out of their bark hides, branching horns, or magnificent bole backbones. Few that fell trees plant them; nor would planting avail much towards getting back anything like the noble primeval forests. During a life-time only saplings can be grown, in the place of the old trees — tens of centuries old — that have been destroyed.

It took more than three thousand years to make some of the trees of these Western woods — trees that are still standing in perfect strength and beauty — waving and singing in the mighty forests of the Sierra. Through all the wonderful, eventful centuries since Christ's time — and long before that — God has cared for these trees, saved them from drought, disease, avalanches, and a thousand straining, leveling tempests and floods; but he cannot save them from fools.

By the time "Any Fool Can Destroy Trees" came out, John Muir had been acknowledged as the most ardent defender of the American wilderness. In 1876 he urged the federal government to adopt a forest conservation policy and he was largely responsible for the establishment of Sequoia and Yosemite National Parks in 1890.

☾*

CANTICLE OF BROTHER SUN

Saint Francis of Assisi

Most High, all powerful, all good Lord!
All praise is yours, all glory, all honor, and all blessing.
To you alone, Most High, do they belong.
No mortal lips are worthy to pronounce your name.

All praise be yours, my Lord, through all you have made,
And my first lord, Brother Sun,
Who brings the day; and light you gave us through him.
How beautiful is he, how radiant in all his splendor!
Of you, Most High, he bears the likeness.

All praise be yours, my Lord, through Sister Moon and Stars;
In the heavens you have made them bright and precious and fair.

All praise be yours, my Lord, through Brother Wind and Air,
And fair and stormy, all the weather's moods.
To everyone who breaths, you give a share.

All praise be yours, my Lord, through Sister Water,
So useful, lowly, precious and pure.

All praise be yours, my Lord, through Brother Fire,
Through whom you lighten up the night.
How beautiful is he, how bright! Full of power and strength.

All praise be yours, my Lord, through Sister Earth, our mother,
Who feeds us in her sovereignty and produces abundant fruits
     and colored flowers and herbs.

On a pilgrimage to Rome, Francis (1182–1226), son of a wealthy cloth merchant, was moved by compassion at the sight of beggars in Saint Peter's Square. Immediately he exchanged his clothes with one of them and spent the rest of the day begging for alms. This brief experience of being penniless deeply affected him. Upon his return to Assisi and being disowned by his father, he devoted the rest of his life to serving the poor.

☽*

A LAND of FLOWING STREAMS

Deuteronomy 8

Your gracious God is bringing you into a good land, a land with flowing streams gushing out into the valleys and hills. God is leading you to a land full of wheat and barley, of vines and fig trees and pomegranates, a land of olive trees and honey. It is a land where you will eat bread without scarcity, where you will lack nothing, a land whose stones are iron and from whose hills you may mine copper. You shall eat your fill and bless your God for the good land the Holy One has given you.

But take care that you do not forget your Creator by failing to keep God's commandments. Do not forget that it was God who led you through the great and terrible wilderness, who made water flow for you from a rock and fed you in the wilderness.

The Hebrews had great affection for the land and they integrated this love with a comprehensive moral framework. In this selection, the Hebrews are entering Canaan, the "Promised Land," a land flowing with milk and honey. The generous God who provides such abundance only requires in return that the people honor the Divine Power and "not forget your Creator by failing to keep God's commandments."

☪*

LOOKING DEEPLY

Thich Nhat Hanh

We need to look deeply at things in order to see. When a swimmer enjoys the clear water of a river, he or she should also be able to *be* the river. If we want to continue to enjoy our rivers — to swim in them, walk beside them, even drink their water — we have to meditate on *being* the river. If we cannot feel the rivers, the mountains, the air, the animals, and other people from within their own perspective, the rivers will die and we will lose our chance for peace.

If you are a mountain climber or someone who enjoys the countryside, or the green forest, you know that the forests are our lungs outside our bodies, just as the sun is our heart outside our bodies. Yet we have been acting in a way that has allowed two million square miles of forest land to be destroyed by acid rain, and we have destroyed parts of the ozone layer that regulate how much direct sunlight we receive. We are imprisoned in our small selves, thinking only of the comfortable conditions of this smaller self, while we destroy our larger self. We need to be able to be our true self. This means being able to *be* the river, to *be* the forest, the sun, and the ozone layer. Thus we will be able to understand and have hope for the future.

According to Thich Nhat Hanh, it is not enough to talk of peace, we need to be *peace. To live our lives connected with the forces of the universe, we need to look deeply into the heart of creation* — to be *the river,* to be *the forest,* to be *the sun and stars. Doing so we will become our true selves and look to the future with hope and expectation.*

☾*

SEEING CREATION THROUGH THE EYES OF THE HOLY ONE

A Meditation of about Two Hours for Anyone, Anytime, Any Place

Quiet Garden in Keats, Kansas

Find a quiet place by yourself.

From where you are, focus on your surrounding environment.

- How many different aspects of God's creation can you observe from this one place?

- Use all your senses — look, listen, smell, and touch.

- Write down everything you observe. Don't be concerned about not knowing the names of things.

- Find one particular living thing (plant, insect, bird) that you can closely observe. Write a detailed description of it, noting everything you can observe. Include its relationships with its environment. Be as detailed as possible.

Meditate on the scriptural truth that you are God's appointed caregiver of that living thing you have just described.

🦋   How has your observation affected how you think about your responsibility as a caregiver toward that small piece of God's creation?

Read Psalm 148.

Take some time to pray, thanking and praising God for the creation surrounding you.

The evening shadows are falling across the prairie grassland. As the hush of the day recedes, the tall grasses are highlighted against the golden setting sun. Welcome to the Quiet Garden, a tall grass nature preserve, in Keats, Kansas. This selection, passed out to visitors to this rural refuge, is a meditative exercise to help visitors appreciate God's creation in the Quiet Garden.

C*

TO WHOM DOES THE EARTH BELONG?

Al-Hafiz B. A. Masri

There are so many stars and planets in the heavens that it is impossible to count them. Yet, in all those heavenly bodies we have not been able to find anything that has life, except on our planet Earth. Even here there are so many different species of living creatures and animals that it is impossible to count them. Yet, out of the millions of kinds of living beings, we are the only species who have the brains to understand the difference between right and wrong in the moral sense and who can use the power of our minds to choose between the two.

It is only because of this freedom of choice that we are considered to be higher in rank than the other animals. Animals, too, possess minds and can distinguish between what is good and bad. However, their brains are not developed enough to distinguish between virtue and sin. Our freedom of choice, based on knowledge and intelligence, puts on us the added responsibility of caring for the rest of God's creation and for those very resources of nature which help all kinds of life on earth to stay alive.

The laws of nature were laid down and are enforced by the Supreme Controller we call God (Allah in Arabic). The universe is God's scheme; God knows what is needed to run it and weighs and measures everything accordingly. The Koran tells us:

Have they never cast a glance at the firmament above? How we
have set it up and decked it out! And how there are no rifts in
it. And the earth — we have spread it out like a carpet; we
have cast on it firm mountains and caused it to grow, in pairs,
all kinds of palatable vegetation. All this merits deep reflection. (Koran 50:6-8).

It is God who created the heavens and the earth, according to
a plan and with a purpose. Whatever God wills to *Be*, it
evolves into *Being* — God's words turn into reality. (Koran
6:73)

According to the Koran, the universe, including the earth, was created in
six eons, meaning six ages of the universe, or six stages:

Have not the incredulous people considered that the heavens
and the earth were originally one closed-up mass, and we rent
them asunder? Do not they know that it is out of water that
we have made everything living? (Koran 21:30)

The ecological problems we are facing today arise from the fact that we
have started using very scarce resources wastefully and in such a way that we
are not giving nature a chance to reproduce the things we are taking from it.
We are also consuming nonrenewable resources at a very fast rate. The laws
of nature are based on its own rhythm. We must learn to operate in accor-
dance with that rhythm.

When we study the lives of the early Muslims, we find that they considered all the elements of nature as the common property of all the creatures. Our right to use the natural resources is only in the sense of *usufruct*, which means being given the right to use another person's property on the understanding that we will not damage, destroy, or waste what is in our trust. According to Islamic law, the elements of nature such as land, water, air, fire, forests, and sunlight were considered to be the common property of all, not only of all human beings, but of all creatures. The Islamic rules on this issue are very specific and clear, based on the Koran:

> Ask them: "To whom does the earth and all that it contains belong, if you know." (Koran 23:84)

> To God belongs all that the heavens and earth contain. (Koran 22:64)

God is the Supreme Controller of the universe and it is God who has created it, including our planet Earth for a purpose which God knows best. God has created each and every living being. When our souls are presented to God, we will be judged as to how we have conducted ourselves during our lives on earth. One of the things of which we shall be judged will be the active kindness we have shown to all that God created, as we are told by the Holy Prophet Mohammed in these words:

> All creation is like a family of God and He loves most those who are most beneficent to His family.

The answer to all our problems on earth lies in humanity's total submission to the will of God and in trying to carry out God's will, which is expressed in the laws of nature. That is what the Koran tells us in these words:

> Set your face on true religion — the nature of God on which
> He has instituted the innate nature of mankind. No change is
> permissible in God's creation. This is the eternal religion.
> (Koran 30:30)

Let us try to grasp the true spirit of the eternal word of the Creator before it is too late. "Call to me, and I shall answer." (Koran 40:60)

The Koran, the fourteen-hundred-year-old sacred book of Islam, laid the foundations for all time for the basic nature of transactions between people with each other and with the natural world. Islam understands that spiritual and physical well-being of humanity are dependent upon each other and that both are related to just and cordial relations with all the forces and creatures of nature.

☪*

ON GENESIS

Kwansik Kim

The heaven opened and the earth was there.
"Let there be light," and there was light.
There was evening; there was morning.
This was the first day. The first day was followed
By the second, the third, the fourth, the fifth,
And the sixth ... All things came into being.

The next day, the seventh day,
The Lord closed his eyes and rested in peace.

In the garden which mocks those in exile
Flowers of all kinds bloom and
Birds fly joyfully to the rim of clouds.
But the people miss those fruits in another tree.

Now I hear Jehovah's deep voice ring in my ears
Like a gust of wind and
I cry from the depth of my heart.

Let me go back to the original state
In which you molded me out of clay
And gave me your breath.

Snake, be not jealous again.
Be not jealous of me;
Be not jealous of my wife.

Bound in coils of sorrow
That will not come off like thread,
Melt into the marrow of my bones.

I wish to live like a mole
Just like a mole
Digging earth for a living.

Therefore I testify to the following:
Those who sacrifice their own interests gain the world.
Those who mind their own interests lose the world.

An ancient sage from the Orient teaches us:
Watched by ten eyes, pointed at by ten men's fingers,
How can one shield himself with his own hands
From the millions of burning angry eyes of the watchful world?
In the reign of the Korea dynasty, even Bulgasari[1] in
the capital city of Songdo, invulnerable as the monster
was, was sensible enough to eat metals only.
But Bulgasaries today have no scruples and eat anything
imaginable anywhere imaginable. They do away with the

[1.] A ficticious monster believed to devour metals.

State, parks, and even stretches of sands along the
Han river.[2] They bake bread of sands going yum yum.

Still further
They do away with every sanctuary which our ancestors
Dreaded even to tread in, those gigantic trees
in the primeval forests which never heard the sounds
of ax, let alone were touched by its stroke;
Now the din of power saws wears out our nerves.
Look at those rows and rows of skeletons downed
mercilessly at the hand of civilization.
Deprived of their homes in the green valleys,
Where will those birds and beasts pass the winter?
Have those flocks of crows in the fields fled
Their habitats in Mount Chiri?[3]

The vicious rule of the State poisons those innocent
Animals; God ought to be disturbed and angered in
The recesses of the heavenly kingdom.

I am not stone-blind, nor am I stone-deaf.
Listen, Dictators! I have never known that the dictators
Ever died a natural death.

[2.] A river flowing through Seoul.
[3.] A mountain of 6,300 feet bordering three southern provinces in Korea.

Kwansik Kim (1934–1970) was a high school teacher who wrote poetry and raised sheep on the outskirts of Seoul, Korea. Deeply religious, he was also skeptical of the power of the state and the damage done to the environment in the name of "progress." From his pasture on the edge of the city, the poet thought deep thoughts and wrote verse. Kim was probably like many of us — often fed up with over-stressed, frenetic urban life yet dependent upon it for livelihood.

C*

NATURE WE SEE

Guru Nānak

Nature we see
Nature we hear
Nature we observe with awe, wonder, and joy
Nature in nether regions
Nature in the skies
Nature in the whole creation
Nature in the sacred texts
Nature in all reflection
Nature in food, in water, in garments, and in love for all
Nature in species, kinds, colors
Nature in life forms
Nature in good deeds
Nature in pride and in ego
Nature in air, water, and fire

Nature in the soil of the earth.
All nature is yours, O powerful Creator,
You command it, observe it, and pervade within it.

The Sikh religion, a hybrid between Islam and Hinduism, was founded by Guru Nānak (1469–1539) from the Punjab region of northwest India. Sikhism has been built on the message of the oneness of creation. The Sikh holy book, from which this selection is taken, is called the Guru Granth Sahib. *It collects the wisdom of the first ten gurus of Sikhism.*

☾*

EVERY PART OF THE EARTH IS SACRED

Chief Seattle

Every part of the earth is sacred to my people. Every shining pine needle, every sandy shore, every mist in the dark woods, every meadow, every humming insect. All are holy.

We know the sap that courses through the trees as we know the blood that runs though our veins. We are part of the earth and the earth is part of us. The perfumed flowers are our sisters. The bear, the deer, the great eagle; these are our brothers. The rocky crests, the berries in the meadow, the body heat of the pony and the people, all belong to the same family.

The shining water that moves in the streams and rivers is not just water but the blood of our ancestors. Each shimmering reflection in the clear water of the lakes tells of events and memories in the life of my people. The water's murmur is the voice of my father's father.

The rivers are our brothers. They quench our thirst. They carry our canoes and give drink to our children. So you must give the rivers the kindness you would give any brother or sister.

The air is precious to us. The air shares its spirit with all the life it supports. The wind that gave our grandfather his first breath also receives his last sigh. The wind also gives our children the spirit of life.

The earth is our mother. What befalls the earth befalls all the children of the earth. All things are connected like the blood that connects us all. We did not weave the web of life, we are merely strands in it. Whatever we do to the web, we do to ourselves.

This we know: that our god is also your god. The earth is precious to God and to harm the earth is to heap contempt upon its creator.

What will happen when the buffalo are all slaughtered? The wild horses tamed? What will happen when the secret corners of the forest are heavy with the scent of many people and the view of the ripe hills is blotted by talking wires? Where will the thicket be? Gone! Where will the eagle be? Gone! And what is it to say good-bye to the swift pony and the hunt? The end of living and the beginning of survival.

We love the earth as a newborn loves its mother's heartbeat. Preserve the land for all children and love it, as God loves us all. We Indians are part of this land. You too are part of this land. The earth is precious to us. It is also precious to you. None of us can be apart. We are all brothers and sisters, together woven in to this sacred earth.

Chief Seattle, in this letter written to President Polk in 1852, explains that the holiness of all creation is revealed in the web and unity of mutually dependent relationships.

☾*

TOUCH THE EARTH

Luther Standing Bear

The Lakotas were true naturalists, lovers of nature. They loved the earth and all things of the earth, the attachment growing with age. The old people came literally to love the soil and they sat or reclined on the ground with a feeling of being close to a mothering power. It was good for the skin to touch the earth and the old people liked to remove their moccasins and walk with bare feet on the sacred earth. Their tepees were built on the earth and their altars were made of earth. The birds that flew in the air came to rest upon the earth and it was the final abiding place of all things that lived and grew. The soil was soothing, strengthening, cleansing, and healing.

That is why the old Indians still sit upon the earth instead of propping themselves up and away from its life-giving forces. For them to sit or lie upon the ground is to be able to think more deeply and to feel more keenly; they can see more clearly into the mysteries of life and come closer in kinship to other lives around them. . . .

Kinship with all creatures of the earth, sky and water was a real and active principle. For the animal and bird world there existed a familial feeling that kept the Lakota safe among them and so close did some of the Lakotas come to their feathered and furred friends that in true brotherhood they spoke a common tongue.

The old Lakotas were wise. They knew that a person's heart away from nature would become hard. They knew that lack of respect for growing and living things soon led to lack of respect for humans too. So they kept their youth close to the earth's softening influence.

The Lakota Indian Luther Standing Bear was born in 1868 and grew up on the high plains of what is now the states of North and South Dakota and Nebraska. He later became a chief. In this selection he describes how the Lakota lived in kinship with all living creatures and why people need to touch the earth to be truly wise and truly human.

C*

A REVOLUTION FOR ANIMALS, RIVERS, LAKES, AND TREES

Ernesto Cardenal

In September more coyotes were seen
    round San Ubaldo,
      more alligators shortly after the triumph
    in the rivers near San Ubaldo,
      more rabbits in the road and grisons…
The bird population has tripled, they say,
    especially the tree duck.
The noisy ducks fly down to swim
    where they see the water shining.

Somoza's men also destroyed
    lakes, rivers, and mountains.
    They diverted rivers for their estates.
The Ochomogo dried up last summer.

The Sinecapa dried
    because of the great landowners' tree-felling.
The Matagalpa Rio Grande ran dry during the war,
    over the plains of Sebaco.
They built two dams on the Ochomogo
    and capitalist chemical waste
crashed into the river
    whose fish staggered like drunks.

The River Boaco has filthy water.
The Moyuá lagoon dried up. A Somoza colonel
    stole the lands from the peasants and built a dam.
The Moyuá lagoon for centuries so lovely where it lay.
    But now the little fishes will come back.

Few iguanas rest in the sun, few armadillos.
Somoza sold the green Caribbean turtle.
They exported sea turtle and iguana eggs in lorries.
    The caguama turtle is becoming extinct.

José Somoza has been putting an end
    to the sawfish in the Great Lake.
Extinction threatens the ocelot
    with its soft wood-colored pelt,
and the puma and the tapir in the mountains,
    like the peasants in the mountains.

And poor River Chiquito! Its disgrace
    shames the whole country.
    Somoza's ways of befouling its waters.
The River Chiquito of León, is choked with sewage,
    and effluent from soap and tanning factories,
    white waste from soap, red from tanneries,
    its bed bestrewn with plastic junk,
    chamber pots and rusty iron.
That was Somoza's legacy.
We must see it running clear and sweet again,
    singing its way to the sea.

All Managua's filthy water is in Lake Managua
    and chemical waste,
    and all over Solentiname.
On the isle of La Zanta, lies a big white heap
    of stinking sawfish bones.

But now the sawfish and the freshwater shark
    can breathe again.
Once more Tisma's waters mirror many herons.
It has lots of little grackles,
    garganeys, tree ducks, kiskadees.

And flowers are flourishing.
Armadillos are very happy with this government.

We are recovering forests, streams, lagoons.
We are going to decontaminate Lake Managua.

Not only humans longed for liberation.
All ecology groaned.
The revolution
    is also for animals, rivers, lakes, and trees.

Now esteemed a hero of the Sandinista revolution, the Roman Catholic priest and poet Ernesto Cardenal (born in 1925 in Granada, Nicaragua) was once considered a dangerous enemy by Nicaragua's ruling Somoza family who owned five million acres of lands, most of it illegally acquired. He taught the people the simple message: love your neighbor, know your legal rights, and be proud of your Indian heritage. According to Cardenal, not only do the people need a revolution to restore true justice to creation, but a revolution is likewise needed for animals, rivers, lakes, and trees.

C*

AND GOD BECAME AN INDIAN

José Gómez

Yes, they were and are with us,
but we barely noticed them.
Carrying their heavy loads on the outskirts of the markets.

Selling fruits and vegetables from sunrise to sunset,
     submerged in mud, breathless, sweating,
     laying the foundations of tall buildings,
     their hand held out: "Alms. For the love of God."

As if Atahualpa, Rumiñahui, Guayas, and Quail[1]
were nothing to these people.
     As if they were others.
Never did it occur to us that these were their offspring.
Beasts of burden, dirty, lying, drunk, thieving.
At best, quaint.

This May 28th the veil covering our eyes began to fall.
A growing clamor began to be heard.
There, in Santo Domingo, not on the island of Española,
     but rather, in the church in Quito.
Subsequently, footpaths, highways, bridges, hills, and ravines
donned red ponchos, black ponchos, white blouses,
     sombreros, necklaces, boots, and espadrilles.

Tens of thousands descended upon Riobamba
and once there shouted, "ENOUGH!"

For the hour had arrived to uncover the cover-up,

[1.] Indian leaders during the conquest.

to call things by their name:
     invasion, conquest, extermination.
To examine history through their eyes.
To illuminate the present with the past.
That's how we can begin to see clearly, to understand:
that if they died by the tens of thousands before
by sword and by fire,
of hunger and of plague,
a bloody holocaust for the God of Power, the God of Wealth,
to this day we continue to kill thus.
The potato which we eat each day,
their handicrafts a thousand-fold
     exude pain and anguish.

That veil covering their eyes began to fall.
Memory dispossessed forgetting,
admiration replaced contempt.
From being teachers, we became students.
Students of love for the land which we destroyed,
of the community, which we,
     children of the God of community, had lost.

Students of His active nonviolence,
     which frees without destruction,
     as proven centuries over.

This Christmas Eve, I am going to dream
that the Son of God has been born amongst us once again.
And his face is one of an Indian.

The five-hundredth anniversary of the arrival of Christopher Columbus in 1992 was a time for the people of the Americas to assess the meaning of his "discovery." The "dream" of Ecuadorian poet José Gómez was that the Holy Child, born to carry the sufferings of the world, will this Christmas bear the face of an Indian, and bring a new sense of awareness to the world.

☽*

MINDFUL VERSES

Thich Nhat Hanh

A way to help us dwell in the present moment is to practice reciting *gathas*, or mindful verses. When we focus our mind on a *gatha*, we return to ourselves and become more aware of each action. When the *gatha* ends, we continue our activity with heightened awareness. When we practice with *gathas* the *gathas* and the rest of our life become one, and we live our entire lives in awareness. We find that we have more peace, calm, and joy which we can share with others.

Waking up this morning, I smile.

Twenty-four new hours are before me.
I vow to live fully in each moment
and to look at all beings with the eyes of compassion.

What better way to start the day than with a smile? Your smile affirms your awareness and determination to live in peace and joy. How many days slip by in forgetfulness? What are you doing with your life? Look deeply and smile. The source of a true smile is an awakened mind.

How can you remember to smile when you wake up? You might hang a reminder — such as a branch, a leaf, a painting, or some inspiring words — in your window or from the ceiling above your bed so that you notice it when you wake up. Once you develop the practice of smiling, you may not need a sign. You will smile as soon as you hear a bird sing or see the sunlight stream through the window. Smiling helps you approach the day with gentleness and understanding.

Walking on the earth
is a miracle!
Each mindful step
reveals the wondrous Dharmakaya[1]

Dharmakaya has come to mean the essence of all that exists. All phenomena — the song of a bird, the warm rays of the sun, a cup of hot tea — are

---

[1.] Dharmakaya means the "body" *(kaya)* of Buddhist teaching, which is Dharma: righteousness, justice, virtue, harmony, the unity of life. It is living with the unity of life, speaking kindly, acting kindly, living not just for one's self but for the welfare of all.

manifestations of Dharmakaya. This poem can be recited as we get out of bed and our feet touch the floor. It can be used during walking meditation or any time we stand up and walk.

Walking on the earth is a miracle. We do not have to walk in space or on water to experience a miracle. The real miracle is to be awake in the present moment. Walking on the green earth, we can realize the wonder of being alive.

> Opening the window,
> I look out on to the Dharmakaya.
> How wondrous is life!
> Attentive to each moment,
> My mind is clear like a calm river.

We, too, are of the same nature as those wonders of the universe.

> Water flows from high in the mountains.
> Water runs deep in the earth.
> Miraculously, water comes to us,
> and sustains all life.

Even if we know the source of our water, we still take its appearance for granted. But it is thanks to water that life is possible. Our bodies are more than 70 percent water. Our food can be grown and raised because of water. Water is a good friend which nourishes many thousands of species on earth. Its benefits are numberless.

Reciting this *gatha* before turning on the tap or drinking a glass of water enables us to see the stream of fresh water in our own hearts so that we feel completely refreshed. To celebrate this gift of water is to cultivate awareness and help sustain life and the lives of others.

> Water flows over these hands.
> May I use them skillfully
> to preserve the planet.

Our beautiful earth is endangered. We are about to exhaust its resources by polluting its rivers, lakes, and oceans, thus destroying the habitats of many species, including our own. We are destroying the forests, the ozone layer, and the air. Because of our ignorance, fears, and hatred of one another, our planet may be destroyed as an environment hospitable to life.

The earth stores water, and water gives life. Observe your hands as the water runs over them. Do you have enough clear insight to preserve and protect this beautiful planet, our Mother Earth?

> This plate of food,
> so fragrant and appetizing,
> also contains much suffering.

This *gatha* has its root in a Vietnamese folk song. When we look at our plate, filled with fragrant and appetizing food, we should be aware of the bitter pain of people who suffer from hunger. Every day, forty thousand children die as a result of hunger and malnutrition. Every day! Looking at our plate we "see" Mother Earth, the farm workers, and the tragedy of hunger and malnutrition.

Before a meal, we can join our palms in mindfulness and think about the children who do not have enough to eat. Slowly and mindfully we breathe three times and recite this *gatha*. Doing so will help us maintain mindfulness. Perhaps one day we will find ways to live more simply in order to have more time and energy to do something to change the systems of injustice in the world.

> I entrust myself to the earth;
> Earth entrusts herself to me.
> I entrust myself to the Holy One;
> The Holy One entrusts herself to me.

To plant a seed or a seedling is to entrust it to the earth. The plant takes refuge in the earth. Whether it grows well or not depends upon the earth. Whether the earth is beautiful, fresh and green or withered and dry depends upon the plants entrusted to the earth. The plants and the earth rely on each other for life. Life relies on life and all life is connected in the golden web of life.

The Buddhist approach to harmony and peace is infused with a spirit of reverence for all of life. It is brought about by an attitude of mindful awareness. The doors to mindfulness are opened through quiet, calm breathing and emptying the mind of all except what is present right now and opening the eyes of the soul to let the present moment speak to its depths. Mindfulness does not come naturally to human beings; it is an art to be cultivated.

C*

NATURE

Ralph Waldo Emerson

If one would be alone, let him look at the stars. The rays that come from those heavenly worlds will separate him and what he touches. One might think the atmosphere was made transparent with this design, to give to humanity, in the heavenly bodies, the perpetual presence of the sublime. Seen in the streets of cities, how great they are! If the stars should appear one night in a thousand years, how would people believe and adore; and preserve for many generations the remembrance of the city of God which has been shown! But every night come out these envoys of beauty, and light the universe with their admonishing smile.

The stars awaken a certain reverence, because though always present, they are inaccessible; but all natural objects make a kindred impression, when the mind is open to their influence. Nature never wears a mean appearance. Neither does the wise one exhort her secret, and lose her curiosity by finding all her perfection. Nature never becomes a toy to a wise spirit. The flowers, the animals, the mountains, reflected the wisdom of her best hour, as much as they delighted the simplicity of her childhood.

When we speak of nature in this manner, we have a distinct but most poetical sense in the mind. We mean the integrity of impression made by manifold natural objects. It is this which distinguishes the stick of timber of the wood-cutter from the tree of the poet. The charming landscape which I saw this morning is made up of some twenty or thirty farms. Miller owns this field, Locke that, and Manning the woodland beyond. But none of them owns the landscape. There is a property in the horizon which no man has but he whose eye can integrate all the parts. This is the best part of these men's farms, yet to this their warranty deeds give no title.

To speak truthfully, few adult persons can see nature. Most persons do not see the sun. At least they have a superficial seeing. The sun illuminates only the eye of the adult, but shines into the eye and the heart of the child. The lover of nature is the one whose inward and outward senses are still truly adjusted to each other; who has retained the spirit of infancy even into the era of adulthood. Such a person's intercourse with heaven and earth becomes part of her daily food. In the presence of nature a wild delight runs through the person, in spite of real sorrows. Nature says — this is my creature, with all his impertinent griefs, he shall be glad with me. Not the sun or the summer alone, but every hour and season yields its tribute of delight; for every hour and change corresponds to and authorizes a different state of the mind, from breathless noon to grimmest midnight.

Nature is a setting that fits equally well a comic or one in mourning. In good health, the air is a cordial, full of incredible virtue. Crossing a bare common, in snow puddles, at twilight, under a clouded sky, without having in my thoughts any occurrence of special good fortune, I have enjoyed perfect exhilaration. I am glad to the brink of fear. In the woods too, a woman casts off her years, as the snake its skin, and at what period so ever of life is always a child. In the woods is perpetual youth.

Within these plantations of God, a decorum and sanctity reign, a perennial festival is dressed, and the guest sees not how he should tire of them in a thousand years. In the woods we return to reason and faith. There I feel that nothing can befall me in life — no disgrace, no calamity which nature cannot repair. Standing on bare ground — my head bathed by the blithe air and uplifted into infinite space — all mean egoism vanishes. I become a transparent eyeball. I am nothing. I see all. The currents of the Universal Being circulate through me. I am part and parcel of God. The name of the dearest friend sounds foreign and accidental. I am the lover of uncontained and immortal beauty. In the wilderness I find something more dear and connate than in the streets or villages. In the tranquil landscape, and especially in the distant line of the horizon, one beholds something beautiful.

The greatest delight that the fields and woods minister is the suggestion of a relationship between human beings and the natural world. I am not alone and unacknowledged. The trees and plants nod to me and I to them. The waving of the boughs in the storm is new to me and old. It takes me by surprise, and yet is not unknown. Its effect is like that of a higher thought or a better emotion coming over me, when I deemed I was thinking justly or doing right. Yet it is certain that the power to produce this delight does not reside in nature alone, nor in humanity by itself, but in a harmony of both....Nature always wears the colors of the spirit.

Ralph Waldo Emerson, one of New England's leading transcendentalist writer-philosophers of the nineteenth century, wrote "Nature" in 1833. Disappointed in the development of his professional life and following the deaths of his brother and his frail and lovely wife of a year, Ellen, he sought the solace of nature for the healing of his grief. For Emerson, to find comfort for life's hurts and disappointments, to know oneself, to know God, to know genuine beauty, to be in touch with the source of the universe — for all these things solitude in the natural world was essential.

C*

I DREAM…

Mainak Bhusan Banerjee

I dream that on the globe of the next century,
there is
no Christian,
no Muslim,
no Hindu,
no Buddhist,
no Jain,
no Jew,
nothing of that sort,
only *Human Being.*
No nationality,
but only one humanity.

No capitalism,
no socialism,
but only humanism.
No governments,
no high sounding constitutions
but only the United Nations
with its simple clear charter
to work for peace
and a clean
and green globe
where men and women
from
the North Pole
to
the South Pole
and
all around the equator
will
hold one flag
and
sing one anthem.

Mainak Bhusan Banerjee is a teenager from India with a clear eye and a beautiful dream of a green, harmonious world and one united humanity. The health of the world depends upon dreamers, like Mainak, who offer hope to all who seek a healthy, peaceful universe.

☪*

THE PEACEFUL EARTH

Isaiah 11

The wolf shall live with the lamb,
and the leopard with the kid.
The calf and the lion shall feed together.
The cow and the bear will be friends.
Their young shall lie down together.
The lion will eat straw like the ox.
The infant will play safely over the cobra's hole.
The young child shall put its hand on the adder's den.
They will neither hurt nor destroy on all my holy mountain.
For the whole earth will be full of the knowledge
    of our Holy God
        just as the waters cover the sea.

The prophet Isaiah anticipates a time when all humanity and every creature of the natural world will be reconciled, when ancient enemies will be sharing a love feast, when the earth will be "full of the knowledge of our Holy God."

☪

INTO THE MOUNTAINS

John Muir

When I set out on the long excursion that finally led to California, I wandered afoot and alone from Indiana to the Gulf of Mexico, intending to go thence to South America. But I was unable to find a ship bound for South America and decided to visit California for a year or two to see its wonderful flora and the famous Yosemite Valley. All the world was before me and every day was a holiday, so it did not seem important to which one of the world's wildernesses I first should wander.

So on the first of April, 1868, I set out for Yosemite. It was the bloom time of the year over the lowlands and coast ranges; the landscapes of the Santa Clara Valley were drenched with sunshine, all the air was quivering with the songs of meadowlarks, and the hills were so covered with flowers that they seemed to be painted. Slow indeed was my progress through these glorious gardens, the first of the California flora I had seen. I wandered enchanted in long waving curves, knowing by my pocket map that Yosemite Valley lay to the east and that I should surely find it.

Of all the mountain ranges I have climbed, I like the Sierra Nevada the best. Its marvelous beauty, displayed in striking and alluring form, woos the admiring wanderer on and on, higher and higher, charmed and enchanted. Benevolent, solemn, fateful, pervaded with diving light, every landscape glows like a countenance hallowed in eternal repose.

The weather is mostly sunshine embellished with magnificent storms, and nearly everything shines from base to summit — the rocks, streams, lakes, glaciers, irised falls, and the forests of silver fir and silver pine. And how bright is the shining after summer showers and dewy nights, and after frosty nights in spring and autumn, when the morning sunbeams are pouring through the crystals on the bushes and grass, and in winter through the snow-laden trees! Well may the Sierra be called the Range of Light.... Nowhere will you see the majestic operations of nature more clearly revealed.

The Apostle of the American Wilderness, John Muir (1838–1914) emigrated with his family from Scotland to a farm in Portage, Wisconsin, when he was nine years old. After an accident in a factory in Indiana that nearly cost him an eye, Muir reexamined his priorities and in 1869 set out on foot intending to go to South America. Notes from John Muir's first seasons in the Sierra, "Into the Mountains" explains why he never got there. Upon first encountering the Sierra Nevadas, Muir experienced a spiritual awakening that radically changed the direction of his life.

C*

THE EARTH MY DREAM

Margaret Uyanga

I try to close my eyes in sleep
To close them in a peaceful sleep
But so worried and anxious am I
That I toss through the night.

Worried about our mother earth
Whom I visualize crying out in pain.
At the sight of all her children are doing.
I'm filled with anxiety for change.

Still on my restless couch
I dream of a haven,
An ideal planet earth
Of which everyone is proud

A place where all differences
Involving various races are settled peacefully,
Where the deep blue sea flows undisturbed by filth,
Where all in habitants have a right to live and rejoice!

I fancy a haven of love and happiness
Of lush meadow and roses

Filling the air with fragrance
And every heart with joy.

Margaret Uyanga is an eighteen-year-old poet who lives in Tanzania. She has a dream of the earth as "a haven of love and happiness" because in her short lifetime she has seen too much of a living nightmare.

☪*

THE ONCE AND FUTURE PLANET

Ellen

There was once a beautiful planet
With turquoise seas, emerald forests and skies of blue,
And on this planet were born living creatures.
Everything was clean and new
Until something happened.
A new creature standing on two feet appeared.
He had a new thing called intelligence.
He became a master of all the other creatures.
He began building houses to live in,
Bridges to cross rivers never crossed before.
And slowly he started wrecking the beautiful countryside

Until one day, the beautiful planet was a home no more to man.
And it returned to its beautiful old self after a while;
Peaceful, clean and beautiful,
It seemed as if man was just
A passing thing.

Ellen, a Belgian student writing in Children's State of the World Handbook, *takes a long view of life, for she has a vision of the Earth finally returning to a pristine state of paradise.*

☾*

WALKING SO THAT ALL BEINGS MAY BE PEACEFUL

Thich Nhat Hanh

The open air is likely to be cool and clean in the early morning or late evening. No source of energy is more nourishing than pure air. You take in that energy and feel stronger in your body and mind while you practice walking meditation. When you practice regularly, your life will be gradually transformed. Your movements will be more easygoing, not precipitous, and you will be more aware of what you are doing. In your social relationships and in your making decisions, you will find yourself acting calmly and incisively, with better insight and more compassion. All beings, from the near to the far, large and small — from the moon and the stars to the leaves and the caterpillars — will become peaceful as you take your steps.

Such basic activities as walking and breathing can become the pathways to greater mindfulness. They help us embrace the energy to be here right now and to witness deeply everything that happens in the present moment.

C*

TAKE ONE LAST LOOK

Adita Charda

Take a seat under a tree
and let the stillness envelop you.
Let the liana softly stroke your hair
as you watch patches of sunlight
dancing on the fallen leaves.

Listen carefully and you will hear
the gurgling of a nearby stream,
the chat of monkeys
in the branches above you.

Look carefully and you will see
the verdant green of young shoots
straining towards
the sunlight.
You will notice the bright
splashes of tiny red and
yellow flowers.

Look long and hard,
for you will want to be able to remember
and describe this to your grandchildren
when you return many years from now
and find a bare,
arid desert.

Dissatisfied with the results of the United Nations Conference on Environment and Development in 1992, members of UNICEF asked young people from every corner of the world what they felt the conference should have achieved and what they thought about the future of Mother Earth. Adita Charda, a young woman from Tanzania, expressed her feelings in this poem.

☾*

DEATH

Aleksandra Warzecka

Crushed by burden of lead
    I breathe in the black particles of
    invisible death.
    They are surrounding me,
    surrounding me from all sides.
I keep them away
    with the movement of my hand.
I don't see them but
    they are still in a terrible nearness,
    hidden in mysterious words:
    doxins,
    phenol,
    nitrogen oxides.
Death is lurking,
    encircling every particle of air.
It kills and kills cruelly
    with a black chain which surrounds
    my head,
    my hands,
    my mind.
Death comes with acid rain,
    turning our world into something monstrous:

mutated trees,
    dead animals,
    black dust swirling over my head.
I am looking for the greenness
    and for the normal trees,
    people unchanged into crazies.
But only the black smoke do I have in sight,
    clouds heavy with poison.
    there is invisible death lurking in them,
    invisible death,
    invisible death.
    DEATH.

Anyone traveling through Eastern Europe after the collapse of the Berlin Wall would understand exactly what Aleksandra Warzecka, a seventeen-year-old Polish boy, is talking about. To break this invisible chain of death, according to Lester Brown, president of the World Watch Institute, "depends on more of us becoming environmental activists, working on behalf of the future of the planet and our children."

☾*

WIDENING OUR CIRCLE OF COMPASSION

Albert Einstein

A human being is part of the whole...the universe. We experience thoughts and feelings, as something separated from the rest — a kind of optical delusion of consciousness. The delusion is a kind of prison for us, restricting us to our personal desires and to affection for a few persons nearest to us. Our task must be to free ourselves from this prison by widening our circle of compassion to embrace all living creatures and the whole of nature in its beauty.

Worldwide fame came in 1919 to German-American physicist Albert Einstein (1879-1955) when the theory of relativity that he developed was verified. Two years later he was awarded the Nobel Prize for Physics. In addition to Einstein's ground-breaking work in physics, he was deeply committed to charitable and social organizations that helped resettle large number of refugees arriving in the United States from Nazi Germany.

C*

THINKING GLOBALLY —
A UNIVERSAL TASK

The Dalai Lama

Ancient cultures that have adapted to their natural surroundings can offer special insights on structuring human societies to exist in balance with the environment. For example, Tibetans are uniquely familiar with life on the Himalayan plateau. This has evolved into a long history of a civilization that took care not to overwhelm and destroy its fragile ecosystem. Tibetans have long appreciated the presence of wild animals as symbolic of freedom. A deep reverence for nature is apparent in much of Tibetan art and ceremony. Spiritual development thrived despite limited material progress. Just as species may not adapt to relatively sudden environmental changes, human cultures also need to be treated with special care to insure survival. Therefore, learning about the useful ways of people and preserving their cultural heritage is also a part of learning to care for the environment.

His Holiness Tenzin Gyatso, the XIV Dalai Lama of Tibet, is one of the preeminent spiritual leaders of our time. The occupation of Tibet by the People's Republic of China, the destruction of human rights, and the environment of "The Land of the Snows" forced the Dalai Lama into exile in 1959, and he has been working to restore Tibet to Tibetans ever since. Thus, from personal experience, this humble religious leader knows at firsthand the profound suffering that is the lot of so many of the world's people. He writes with genuine authenticity that transcends barriers of nation and culture.

☪*

WALDEN

Henry David Thoreau

When I wrote the following pages, I lived alone in the woods a mile from any neighbor, in a house which I had built myself, on the shores of Walden Pond, in Concord, Massachusetts, and earned my living by the labor of my hands only. . . .

We may imagine a time when, in the infancy of the human race, some enterprising mortal crept into a hollow in a rock for shelter. Every child begins the world again, to some extent, and loves to stay out doors, even in wet and cold. It plays house as well as horse, having an instinct for it. Who does not remember when young looking at shelving rocks, or any approach to a cave? It was the natural yearning of that portion of our most primitive ancestor which still survived in us. From the cave we have advanced to roofs of palm leaves, of bark and bough, of linen woven and stretched, of grass and straw, of boards and shingles, of stones and tiles. At last we know not what it is to live in the open air, and our lives are domestic in more senses than we think. From the hearth to the field is a great distance. It would be well perhaps if we were to spend more of our days and nights without any obstruction between us and the celestial bodies, if the poet did not speak so much from under a roof, or the saint dwell there so long. Birds do not sing in caves, nor do doves cherish their innocence in dovecotes. . . .

We must learn to reawaken and keep ourselves awake, not by mechanical aids, but by an infinite expectation of the dawn, which does not forsake us in our soundest sleep....

I went to the woods because I wished to live deliberately, to front only the essential facts of life, and see if I could not learn what it had to teach, and not, when I came to die, discover that I had not lived. I wanted to live deep and suck all the marrow out of life....

Time is but a stream I go a-fishing in. I drink at it; but while I drink I see the sandy bottom and detect how shallow it is. Its thin current slides away, but eternity remains. I would drink deeper....

Walk in search of the springs of life....When we walk, we naturally go to the fields and woods. What would become of us if we walked only in a garden or a mall?...

The cutting down of a forest and of all large trees simply deforms the landscape, and makes it more and more tame and cheap....People should burn the fences and let the forest stand!...

I believe in the forest, and in the meadow, and in the night in which the corn grows....The most alive is the wildest....Hope and the future for me are not in lawns and cultivated fields, not in towns and cities, but in the impervious and quaking swamps....A town is saved, not more by the right-eous men in it than by the woods and swamps that surround it....A town-ship where one primitive forest waves above while another primitive forest rots below — such a town is fitted to raise not only corn and potatoes, but poets and philosophers for the coming ages....

Give me the ocean, the desert, or the wilderness. In the desert, pure air and solitude compensate for want of moisture and fertility.... When I would recreate myself, I seek the darkest wood, the thickest and most interminable. I enter a swamp as a sacred place — a *sanctum sanctorum* (the Holy of Holies). Here is the strength and marrow of nature....

In wilderness is the preservation of the world.

If Ralph Waldo Emerson was the most distinguished spirit of the Transcendentalist Movement, Henry David Thoreau (1817–1862), was the movement's most ardent practitioner. Thoreau took up residence at Walden Pond in Concord, Massachusetts, on July 4, 1845. For two years he lived on a tract of land belonging to Emerson, his friend and (in the beginning) mentor. His idea was to strip the life down to its barest essentials and there discover the fundamental laws of nature in their archetypal simplicity.

☪*

WHEN THE LAST LEAF FALLS

Tove

When the last leaf falls,
When the last drop of water dries out,
When the ozone layer is already destroyed,
Will it be too late to understand
that money is not going to save us?

A Holland-based organization, Peace Child International, sent questionnaires to children in sixty countries asking them what an ideal book on the environment would contain. The result was the 1992 publication of the Children's State of the World Handbook, *a colorful book full of children's drawings, poems, essays, and suggestions for improving the quality of Planet Earth. Tove, a young person from Sweden, contributed this poem.*

☾*

AS YOU LEAVE EDEN BEHIND YOU

Central Conference of American Rabbis

Of all created things the source is one,
Simple, single as love; remember
The cell and seed of life, the sphere

That is, of child, white bird, and small blue dragonfly,
Green fern, and the gold four-petalled tormentilla
The ultimate memory.
Each latent cell puts out a future,
Unfolds its differing complexity
As a tree puts forth leaves, and spins a fate
Fern-traced, bird-feathered, or fish-scaled.
Moss spreads its green film on the moist peat,
The germ of dragonfly pulses into animation and takes wing
As the water lily from the mud ascends on its ropy stem
To open a sweet white calyx to the sky.

Humankind has further to travel from simplicity,
From archaic moss, fish, and lily parts,
And into exile travels a long way.

As you leave Eden behind you, remember your home,
For as you remember back into your own being
You will not be alone; the first to greet you
Will be those children playing by the stream,
The otters will swim up to you in the bay,
The wild deer on the moor will run beside you.
Recollect more deeply, and the birds will come,
Fish rise to meet you in their silver shoals,
And darker, stranger, more mysterious lives
Will throng about you at the source
Where the tree's deepest roots drink from the abyss.

Nothing in the abyss is alien to you.
Sleep at the tree's root, where the night is spun
Into the stuff of worlds, listen to the winds,
The tides, and the night's harmonies, and know
All that you knew before you began to forget,
Before you became estranged from your own being,
Before you had too long parted from those other
More simple children, who have stayed at home
In meadow and island and forest, in sea and river.
Earth sends a mother's love after her exiled child,
Entrusting her message to the light and air,
The wind and waves that carry your ship, the rain that falls,
The birds that call to you, and all the shoals
That swim in the natal waters of her ocean.

"As You Leave Eden behind You" is an invitation to us all to reach back to our archaic
roots to the dawn of humanity, to *"recollect more deeply... where the trees deepest roots drink
from the abyss."* Echoing through this selection is the idea of exile and the call to come home to
basic simplicities of being.

C*

THE GOLDEN THREAD

William Willoya and Vinson Brown

We have seen the golden thread, the day of the awakening of the Indian peoples and the formation of a New World of justice and peace, of freedom and God. We have seen how the Warriors of the Rainbow — the new teachers — are prophesied to come and spread this great Message over all the earth.

The world is sick today because it has turned away from the Great Spirit. When people turn once more to the Ancient Being with love and world understanding, the earth will become beautiful again. Indians can help humankind to return to the Wise One Above by obeying the following principles.

Like the great Indians of old, they will teach unity, love, and understanding among all people. They will listen no more to the little people who say they alone have the truth, but shall see that the Great Spirit who listens to all is too big for little things, too full of justice to accept but one self-chosen people, too free to be caged by any mind. They will listen to those who teach harmony between all people, even as the wind blows without favoritism into all the corners of the world.

Like the pure Indians of old, they will pray to the Spirit with a love that flows through every world even as the breeze sings its song to the Silent One among the needles of the pines. In solitude and in council their hearts will lift with joy, free to love everyone as sisters and brothers. As the Great Spirit loves a smile and happiness, they shall sing of the coming glorious union of all humanity.

Like the Indians of the past, by their joy, by their laughter, their love, and their understanding, they shall change all people whom they meet. Like the rushing torrent of a river that wears away the hardest rocks, they shall wear away the hardest hearts with love, until the whole world begins to bloom.

Like the radiant Indians of old who strengthened their muscles by hard exercise and then nourished their souls by fasting and prayer, so shall they make themselves heroes of the new age, conquering every difficulty with the strength of their bodies, the fire of their love and the purity of their hearts. They shall run to the hilltops to pray and fast and into the solitude of the forest and desert to find strength.

Like the Indians of old who let their children run free in the prairies, the woods, and the mountains to help them grow into men and women worthy of their Creator, so the Warriors of the Rainbow today shall work to bring to all children the blessings of the wild, the delight of bare feet running through green grass over the hills, and the cool touch of the wind in their hair. The spiritual civilization that is coming will create beauty by its very breath, turning the waters of rivers clear, building forests and parks where there are now deserts and slums, and bringing back the flowers to the hillsides. What a glorious fight to change the world to beauty!

Like the Indians of old who loved, understood, and knew the powers of animals and plants, who when they killed took no more than they needed for food and clothing, so the Indians of today will brighten the understanding of the ignorant destroyers. They will soften the hearts of the would-be killers so the animals will once more replenish the earth, and the trees shall once again rise to hold the precious soil. On that day all peoples of the earth shall be able to walk in wilderness flowing with life, and the children will see about them the young fawns, the antelope, and the wildlife as of old. Conservation of all that is beautiful and good is a cry woven into the very heart of the new age.

Like the kind Indians of old who gave work to all and kept care of the poor, the sick, and the weak, so the Warriors of the Rainbow shall work to build a new world in which everyone who can work shall work and work with joy and with praise of the Great Spirit. None shall starve or be hurt due to coldness and forgetfulness. No child shall be without love and protection and no old person without help and good companionship in their declining years.

Like the joyful Indians of old, the new Indians shall bring back to their own people and spread to other races the joy of hospitality and kindness and courtesy that made life in the old Indian villages such a happy time for all. How they danced together! How they ate together in loving harmony! How they prayed together and sang together in joy! It shall come again and better in the new world.

Wise Indians shall teach all people to make their deeds count bigger than their words. Deeds of love and kindness and understanding shall change the world.

The wise chiefs are chosen by demonstrating always their quiet love and wisdom in council and their courage in making decisions and working for the common good of all. So shall the Warriors of the Rainbow teach that in the governments of the future, leaders will be chosen out of the ranks by quality alone and then will council together in freedom of thought and conscience. In counsel they shall seek truth and harmony with hearts full of wisdom.

Among the Indians of old, children and youth respected the elders and were taught love and unity, strength of character, love of the Great Chief in the Sky, and good deeds from babyhood. The Warriors of the Rainbow will bring back this lost spirit before it is too late and the youth shall once more do great deeds of selflessness and heroism. The glory and the purity of their lives shall light the world.

Great are the tasks ahead, terrifying are the mountains of ignorance and hate and prejudice, but the Warriors of the Rainbow shall rise as on the wings of the eagle to surmount all difficulties. They will be happy to find that there are now millions of people all over the earth ready and eager to rise and join them in conquering all barriers that bar the way to a new and glorious world! We have had enough now of talk. Let there be deeds.

William Willoya, an Eskimo from Alaska, and Vinson Brown, a Stanford University biology major, traveled throughout the world visiting many indigenous people and studying their thoughts, dreams, and customs. "The Golden Thread" summarizes the teachings they gleaned along the way and challenges us to put our highest ideals into action for the well-being of Planet Earth.

☾*

THE GLORY OF THE FOREST MEADOW IS THE LILY

John Muir

The glory of the forest meadow is the lily. The tallest are from seven to eight feet high with magnificent racemes (stems) of ten to twenty or more small orange-colored flowers. They stand out free in open ground, with just enough grass and other companion plants about them to fringe their feet and show them off to best advantage.

After how many centuries of Nature's care planting and watering them, tucking the bulbs in snugly below winter's frost, shading the tender shoots with clouds drawn above them like curtains, pouring refreshing rain, making them perfect in beauty, and keeping them safe by a thousand miracles. So extravagant is Nature with her choicest treasures, spending plant beauty as she spends sunshine, pouring it forth into land and sea, garden and desert. And so the beauty of lilies falls on angels and men, bears and squirrels, wolves and sheep, birds and bees.

John Muir kept a diary during his first visit to Yosemite and its environs. Forty-one years later, by then a well-established naturalist of national acclaim, Muir was persuaded by his friends to arrange his notes into the book, My First Summer in the Sierra. *This entry was written July 9, 1869.*

☾*

YOU SPREAD OUT THE HEAVENS

Psalm 104

O God, you spread out the heavens like a tent.
    You lay the beams of your chambers in the waters above.
    You make the clouds your chariot.
    You ride on the wings of the wind.

You make the winds your messengers,
    and the flames of fire your couriers.

You have set the earth on its foundations
    so that it shall never be moved.
    You covered it with the deep as with a cloak.
    The waters stood higher than the mountains.

At your rebuke they fled;
    at the voice of your thunder they hastened away.
    They went up into the hills and down to the valleys below,
    to the places you appointed for them.

You set the limits that they should not pass
    so that they shall not cover the earth again.

You make springs gush forth from the valleys, they flow
    between the hills.

All the beasts of the field drink their fill from them,
and the wild asses quench their thirst.
Beside them the birds of the air make their nests
and sing melodies among the branches.

You water your mountains from your dwelling place on high.
The earth is satisfied by the fruit of your work.

You make grass grow for the flocks and herds
and plants for the people's use
that they may bring forth food from the earth
and wine to gladden their spirits,
oil to make their faces shine
and bread to strengthen their hearts.

Your trees are full of sap, the cedars of Lebanon that you planted
in which the birds build their nests and the stork makes its home.
The high hills are a refuge for the mountain goats,
and the stony cliffs for the rock conies.

You appointed the moon to mark the seasons
and the sun knows the time of its setting.
You make darkness and it is night
when the wild beasts of the forest prowl.
The lions roar after their prey, seeking their food from God.
When the sun rises in the morning
they slip away and lie down in their dens.

People go out to their work
   and they labor until evening comes and night is at hand.

O Holy God, how manifold are your works;
   in wisdom you have made them all.
   The earth is full of your creatures.

Yonder is the great and wide sea
   with its living things too numerous to count,
   creatures both small and great.
   There move the ships and there swims the Leviathan[1]
   that you formed.

All the creatures of the earth look to you
   to give them their food in due season.
   You give it to them and they gather it up.
   You open your hand and they are filled with good things.

When you hide your face they are terrified.
   When you take their breath away they die and return to the dust.

You send forth your spirit and they are created
   and so you renew the face of the earth.

[1.] Leviathan: A sea monster, perhaps a whale.

May the glory of the Holy God endure forever;
>   may the Sovereign of heaven and earth rejoice in all his works.
>   God looks on the earth and it trembles, touches the mountains they
>   smoke.

Let us sing to God as long as we live.
>   Let us sing the Holy One's praise as long as we have breath.

"O God, You Spread out the Heavens" is a paraphrase of Psalm 104 in praise of God the Creator of all. Notice that the psalmist is writing about a God who is creating right now — not a remote, past, or passive deity but a God of the present who currently is creating and sustaining the universe. The creation of the world was not a once and for all occurrence; creation continues the divine project of creativity — right now and to eternity.

☾*

A NEW HEAVEN AND A NEW EARTH

Isaiah 65

I am about to create new heavens and a new earth. The former things shall not be remembered or come to mind. Be glad and rejoice forever in what I am creating; for I am about to create Jerusalem as a joy, and its people as a delight. I will rejoice in Jerusalem, and delight in my people; no more shall the sound of weeping be heard in it, or the cry of distress. No more shall there be an infant who lives but a few days, or an old person who does not live out a lifetime; for one who dies at a hundred years will be considered a youth, and one who falls short of a hundred will be considered accursed.

People will build houses and inhabit them; they shall plant vineyards and eat their fruit. They shall not build and another inhabit; they shall not plant and another eat; for like the days of a tree shall the days of my people be, and my chosen shall long enjoy the work of their hands.

My people shall not labor in vain, or bear children for calamity. They shall be the offspring blessed by God, and their descendants shall be blessed for all time to come.

Before they call I will answer. While they are yet speaking I will hear. The wolf and lamb shall feed together, the lion shall eat straw like the ox. They shall not hurt or destroy on all my holy mountain.

God, speaking through the Hebrew prophet, Isaiah, presents an image of a new heaven and a new earth in which all creation will be united, renewed, refreshed, and transformed. This idea finds its final restatement in the culminating chapter of the New Testament in which John has a vision of the New Jerusalem: "Then I saw a new heaven and a new earth." (Revelations 21:1)

☪

Chapter 2

PRAYERS

Just as a white summer cloud, in harmony with heaven and earth, freely floats in the blue sky from horizon to horizon following the breath of the atmosphere, in the same way the pilgrim abandons self to the breath of greater life that leads to the farthest horizons.

— Lama Govinda
The Way of the White Clouds

PRAYER OF LOVE, LIGHT, AND POWER

Kurama Temple

O God, beautiful as the moon, warm as the sun, powerful as the earth, bestow your blessings upon us to uplift humankind. In this holy place, grant that peace may defeat discord, unselfishness may conquer greed, sincere words may overcome deceit, and that respect may surmount insults. Fill our hearts with joy, uplift our spirits, and fill our bodies with glory.

Great God of the Universe, Great Light, Great Mover, bestow upon us who gather to worship you, upon those who strive to touch your heart, a new strength and glorious light.

From the bamboo covered mountains bordering Kyoto, Japan, comes this ancient prayer. It is believed that six million years ago, Mao-son, the spirit of the earth and the conqueror of evil, descended upon Mount Kurama from Venus for the salvation of the earth. Mao-son, also known as Sonten, is considered by Kurama Temple Buddhists to be the supreme soul of the universe. In the Sonten trinity, the Spirit of the Moon is love, the Spirit of the Sun is light, the Spirit of the Earth is power. Mao-son and Sonten are now referred to in this prayer simply as "God" and "Great God of the Universe."

☾*

OPENING THE GATE OF THE CLOUDS

Li Po

In the early morning may we climb up to the mountain top.
May we lift up our hands to open the gate of the clouds.
May our spirits soar, expanding into air,
Until they become one with the sky and earth.

Kuo Hsi, the great Chinese landscape painter, could have had this poem by Li Po (701–762) in mind when he was asked why urban people crave the countryside. He replied, "The rustic retreat nourishes their nature. Amid the carefree play of streams and rocks they take delight. They see country fishermen, woodcutters, and hermits, the soaring crane; they hear the crying of the monkeys. The haze, mist and the haunting spirits of the mountains are what human nature seeks and yet can so rarely find."

☾*

THE MORNING IS YOURS

Celtic Prayer

Almighty God, Creator:
The morning is yours, rising into fullness.

The summer is yours, dipping into autumn.
Eternity is yours, dipping into time.
The vibrant grasses,
the scent of flowers,
the lichen on the rocks,
the tang of seaweed.
All is yours.
Gladly we live in this garden of your creating.

The Celts believed that to know God was to know God's creation, to know God's creation was to know God. Nothing in creation was too small to reveal the Creator, not even lichen in the rocks nor the tang of seaweed. Saint Columbanus (ca. 543–615), told the monks of his community: "Understand the creation if you wish to know the Creator.... For those who wish to know the great deep must first review the natural world."

☾*

LORD OF CREATION

Ralph Waldo Emerson

For blue of stream and blue of sky,
Father we thank thee.
For pleasant shade of branches high

Father, we thank thee.
For fragrant air and cooling breeze,
For the beauty of the blooming trees,
Father in heaven, we thank thee.

For this new morning with its light,
Father, we thank thee.
For rest and shelter of the night,
Father we thank thee.
For health and food, for love and friends,
For everything that goodness sends,
Father in heaven, we thank thee.

"Lord of Creation" is a morning prayer of thanksgiving for the past night and the day
ahead. Its author, Ralph Waldo Emerson (1803–1882), was primarily known as a philosopher and an essayist; yet he was also a fine poet and author of several well-known poems,
among them the *"Concord Hymn"* and the love poem, *"Give All to Love,"* in which the poet
exhorts us, *"Give all to love, obey thy heart."*

C*

A PRAYER of ADORATION for CREATION

New York Board of Rabbis

Heavenly God, the morning stars sing together, the heavens rejoice, the earth is glad, and the people of earth chant to you a new song. Joy pervading all the earth comes from you. You biddest the sun to beam over the smiling earth and you light up our hearts with gladness. Whenever our souls rejoice may we learn to feel kinship with all your natural servants and grow aware of your gentle grace flowing within us.

Admit us into your presence in times of joy, O heavenly God. We seek you that our joys may be hallowed with you, that our happiness may be deepened, that we may join the chorus of the universe, lands and oceans, the stars and infinite space in joyous adoration.

This prayer taken from a Jewish prayer book touches the core of Judeo-Christian tradition. God creates a Holy People for a special divine-human relationship with the critical responsibility — unique to human beings — to honor all creation so that we may "join the chorus of the universe."

☾*

TEACH ME TO PRAISE YOU, O GOD

Saint Isidore of Seville

O God, great and wonderful,
who has created the heavens,
dwelling in their light and beauty;
who has made the earth,
revealing yourself in every flower that opens.
Let not my eyes be blind to you,
neither let my heart be dead,
but teach me to praise you,
even as the lark which offers her song at daybreak.

Saint Isidore of Seville (ca. 560–636) is best known for his voluminous writings, most famous of which is Etymologies (Origins), *a vast encyclopedia in that he aimed to write down all existing knowledge. Nonetheless, he had a humble spirit, which is well illustrated in this piece.*

☽*

THE HAND TRANSFORMS NATURE

D. Pedro Casaldaliga, Jaci C. Maraschin, and Milton Nascimento

The Hand transforms nature,
    and brings bread to the table.
The rain along the road,
    transforms grapes into wine.
And God makes himself into food,
    and gives his life for his own.

We bring in our eyes
the waters of the rivers,
the shine of the fish,
the shade of the trees,
the dew of the night,
the surprise of the hunt,
the dance of the winds,
the silver moon...
We bring the world in our eyes.

This selection, written by Latin American liberation theologians Jaci C. Maraschin, D. Pedro Casaldaliga, and Milton Nascimento is the offertory taken from "And God Saw That It Was Good...", a booklet of Brazilian creation liturgies. It would do well as an introduction to any creation or agape liturgy.

C*

IN PRAISE OF CREATION

Fyodor Dostoyevsky

O Holy God,
may we love and respect all your creation,
all the earth and every grain of sand in it.
May we love every leaf,
every ray of your light.
May we love the animals:
you have given them the rudiments of thought and joy untroubled.
Let us not trouble them;
let us not harass them,
let us not deprive them of their happiness,
let us not work against your intentions.
For we acknowledge that to withhold any measure of love from
anything in the universe
is to withhold that same measure from you.

Russian writer Fyodor Dostoyevsky's (1821–1881) penetration into the darkest recesses of the human heart, together with his unsurpassed moments of illumination, has had a profound influence on the twentieth century literary world. This prayer is spoken through the voice of Starets Zosima in The Brothers Karamazov, *one of Dostoyevsky's greatest novels.*

C*

FOR PURITY OF AIR AND WATER

Free Church of Berkeley

O Power of being,
you have spread an envelope
of clean water and air
around this sapphire earth.
Break every chimney,
rust every pipe
which delivers poison
into our living world.
Teach our brothers and sisters
to live invisible on the only planet
we will ever be given.

"For Purity of Air and Water" is one of the "liberation prayers" contained in The Covenant of Peace, *the prayer book of the Free Church of Berkeley, California. This community, which came into being amid the social and political struggles of the 1960s, has bestowed on us a rich reservoir of timely liturgies and prayers. This one reminds us that we live on "the only planet we will ever be given."*

C*

THE WEB OF LIFE

From the Earth Charter

Creating God, in you everything on earth and in the heavens is bound together in perfect harmony. If we lose the sweetness of the waters, we lose the life of the land. If we lose the life of the land, we lose the majesty of the forest. If we lose the majesty of the forest, we lose the purity of the air. If we lose the purity of the air, we lose the creatures of the Earth.

Open our eyes to behold your creation. Create in us a new spirit of awareness of our place in your delicate balance; transform our hearts that we may reclaim our sense of awe and wonder. Quicken our understanding that we may acknowledge our responsibility and strengthen our resolve to work with you for the healing of your creation; through our Holy God, Savior of the world.

"The Web of Life" was adapted from the preamble of Earth Charter, *a document that is the work of the International Coordinating Committee on Religion and the Earth (ICCRE). ICCRE solicited contributions from the great religions of the world to produce the* Earth Charter, *their contribution to the United Nations Conference on Environment and Development held in June, 1992.*

C*

THANKSGIVING DAY

Anne Rowthorn

Blessed are you, O Holy God, Ruler of the Universe. You in your goodness sustain the whole world with grace, loving kindness, and compassion. We thank you that you have sustained us and all our loved ones since last Thanksgiving Day.

Bless the lands and waters, and multiply the harvests of the world. Where there is drought, bring water. Where there is famine, provide food. Where there is hatred and injustice, bring your justice and love. Where there is war, make peace. Let your spirit go forth that it may renew the face of the earth. Show your loving kindness that our land may give her increase; save us from selfish use of what you so freely give, that men and women everywhere may give thanks for your great bounty and loving kindness to every being and element in the universe. Amen.

The board has been laid with the food, floral, and fruit offerings of friends and family. The household, now gathered around the table, pauses to offer their personal thanksgivings for blessings since last Thanksgiving Day. Everyone who wishes, including the children, offers, in short prayer or phrase what they want to thank God for. At the conclusion, one member of the party reads this collect and the feast begins.

C*

FOR THE HARDEST PLACES ON EARTH

World Council of Churches

O God,
we pray for those places in the world
made awful by climatic conditions;
places of intense cold and heat and drought,
places of great hardship and privation,
where man, woman, and beast are constantly endangered
by the elements and environment.
We give thanks for all that sustains them,
and pray that such may be multiplied
in the hands of our great creator God
and all those who serve God's holy name.

"For the Hardest Places on Earth" is taken from an international, ecumenical prayer book published by the World Council of Churches. In an introduction to this prayer we are told that "there are children in Botswana who have never seen rain."

☪

O CREATING GOD WHO SPREADS THE EARTH, FORGIVE US AND LOVE US

Rig-Veda

O Creating God,
who spreads the earth like a carpet for the sun,
like the skin of a sacrificed beast,
listen to our prayer.

O Creating God,
who places the winds in the forests,
puts wings on horses, milk in cows, virtue in human beings,
who puts fish in the waters, sun in the sky, wind in the mountains,

O Creating God,
who tilts the cup of the clouds on the three worlds,
heaven, earth, and middle sky,
lord who drenches fields of barley with rain,

O Creating God,
who floods earth and sky with sweet milk
when hills are clothed with cloud
and the storms come rushing,

We sing to your glory, O Creating God:
You stand in the universe,

You hold it in your power,
You measure the earth with the sun.

We do not question your power, O Wise God,
like shining rivers that flow, and flowing
do not fill the sea
into which they flow....

If we have ever sinned against a friend,
if we have ever sinned against a brother or sister, mother or father,
if we have sinned against neighbor or stranger,
O Forgiving God, forgive us.

If, like gamblers at dice, we have cheated,
cheated knowingly or unknowingly,
O forgiving God, forgive us.
Forgive us, restore us, and love us.

From the Rig-Veda, one of the four core Hindu scriptures, this prayer is to Varuna, the sky god. Hindus understand God as the one supreme principle of the universe who is approached through a variety of names. Hinduism is the world's most ancient religion and the third largest. It does not have one identifiable founder; it is a fusion of historical traditions, which have taken root in the sacred soil of India.

☪

WHEN SPRING COMES

Zuñi Prayer

When our Earth Mother is replete with living waters,
When spring comes,
The source of our flesh,
All the different kinds of corn,
We shall lay to rest in the ground.
With the Earth Mother's living waters,
They will be made into living beings.
Coming out standing into the daylight
Of their Father Sun,
Calling for rain,
To all directions they will stretch out their hands.
Then from wherever the rain makers stay quietly
They will send forth their misty breath;
Their massed clouds filled with water will come out to sit down with us;
Far from their homes,
With outstretched hands of water they will embrace the corn,
Stepping down to caress them with their fresh waters,
With their fine rain caressing the earth,
And yonder, wherever the roads of the rain makers come forth,
Torrents will rush forth,
Mountains will be washed out,
Logs will be washed down,
Yonder all the mossy mountains

Will drip with water.
The clay-lined hollows of our Earth Mother
Will overflow with water,
From all the lakes
Will rise the cries of the children of the rain makers,
In all the lakes there will be joyous dancing —
Desiring that it should be thus,
I send forth my prayers.

This Zuñi prayer welcomes the new season. The universal polarities known in the Asian world as yin/yang are, elsewhere as feminine/masculine are named Mother Earth/Father Sun. The classic poetic theme of the coming of spring transcends all time, cultures, and traditions. The unidentified Zuñi poet, writing with great grace and beauty, prays that when the spring rains descend upon the expectant earth "there will be joyous dancing."

☾*

I BELIEVE

A Creation Affirmation of Faith

Anne Rowthorn

We believe in the God of all creation,
the maker of heaven and earth,

of sun and moon,
of planets and bright shining stars,
of earth and water,
of every living thing,
of all that is, seen and unseen,
of all that was and is and is to come.

We believe in Jesus Christ,
God's Son in human flesh who stands beside us.
Born of a woman and servant of the poor, he was despised.
Rejected and nailed to a tree,
he suffered and died a cruel death.
On the third day he rolled back the rock
and rose from the tomb.
He ascended into heaven and he is now everywhere present
throughout all creation. He is judging the living and the dead and his
     reign of justice will never end.

We believe in the Holy Spirit, the giver of life,
God's breath within us and scattered throughout the universe.
Creating God, Jesus the Christ, Holy Spirit — Triune God —
you are worshipped and glorified.
You spoke through the prophets before us,
you speak through prophets among us now,
you are source of judgment, the forgiveness of our sins
and the healing of all creation.

We look for restoration of the beauty of your creation,
the resurrection of the dead
and the life of the world to come. Amen.

This work came about when I gave myself the same assignment I gave the students. They (and I) wrote statements of belief that contained all the standard elements of the creeds of their denominations and added references to the environment and the restoration of creation. The idea was to create a creed they could use in their churches as a part of creation liturgies, harvest festivals, environmental Sabbath celebrations, and the like.

☾*

THE RAINBOW COVENANT

Martin Palmer

Brothers and sisters in creation, we covenant this day with you and with all creation yet to be:

> with every living creature and all that contains and
> > sustains you;
> with all that is on earth and with the earth itself;
> with all that lives with the waters and with the waters them-
> > selves;
> with all that flies in the sky and with the sky itself.

We establish this covenant, that all our powers will be used to prevent your destruction.

We confess that it is our kind who put you at the risk of death.

We ask for your trust and as a symbol of our intention we mark our covenant with you by the rainbow.

This is the sign of the covenant between ourselves and every living thing that is found on the earth.

"The Rainbow Covenant" is inspired by the familiar Biblical story of God's promise to Noah after the flood. In Genesis 9:11–13, God assured Noah that "never again will all living beings be destroyed by a flood and never again will a flood destroy the earth. As a sign of this everlasting covenant which I am making with you and with all living creatures, I am putting my rainbow in the clouds. It will be a sign of my covenant with the world."

C*

HYMN TO THE EARTH

Atharva-Veda

O Mother, with your oceans, rivers, and other bodies of water,
    you give us land to grow grains on which our survival depends.
    Please give us as much milk, fruits, water, and cereals
        as we need to eat and drink.

O Mother, bearing folk who speak different languages,
    and follow different religions,
    treating them all as residents of the same house,
    please pour, like a cow who never fails,
    a thousand streams of treasure to enrich us.

May you, our motherland, on whom grow wheat, rice, and barley,
    on whom are born five races of humanity,
    be nourished by the clouds,
    and loved by the rain.

"Hymn to the Earth" from the Atharva-Veda, is an excellent illustration of the Hindu belief all religions are expressions of eternal truth. The Creator God has many faces and no one tradition can of itself see the whole reality of God. In this hymn, the feminine God is compared to a cow who never fails to nourish her children with "a thousand streams of treasure."

☾*

GRANDFATHER, GREAT SPIRIT

Lakota Indian Prayer

Grandfather, Great Spirit,
you have always been, and before you nothing has been.
There is no one to pray to but you.
The star nations all over the heaven are yours,
and yours are the grasses of the earth.
You are older than all need, older than all pain and prayer.

Grandfather, Great Spirit,
fill us with light.
Give us strength to understand and eyes to see.
Teach us to walk the soft earth as relatives to all that live.
Help us, for without you we are nothing.

In this elegant invocation, the Lakota Indian poet calls upon the Grandfather — Great Spirit or God by whatever name we call the Holy One — to teach us to regard the earth with the tenderness and affection we would accord our own mothers, for the Good Earth is the life-giver and sustainer of all. It nourishes every living being.

☾*

MOUNTAIN CHANT

Navajo Chant

The voice that beautifies the land!
The voice above,
The voice of the thunder,
Among the dark clouds
Again and again it sounds,
The voice that beautifies the land!

The voice that beautifies the land!
The voice below,
The voice of the grasshopper,
Among the flowers and grasses
Again and again it sounds,
The voice that beautifies the land!

The "Mountain Chant" with its many variations, is a chant of the beautyway (life span), which is sung for several purposes. It is part of the puberty rite performed with Navajo children when they come of age. It is sung while traveling anywhere but especially over the mountains, as a prayer that the traveler will be at one with the birds and animals, with the rocks and grasses, with the sky and clouds along the way. It is chanted when a person is out of balance with life and needs to be brought back in harmony with the universe.

☾*

AN INDIAN PRAYER

Tom White Cloud

O Great Spirit, whose voice I hear in the winds and whose breath gives life to all the world: hear me. I am one of your many children. I am small and weak. I need your strength and wisdom. Let me walk in beauty and make my eyes ever to behold the red and purple sunset. Make my hands respect the things you have made, my ears sharp to hear your voice. Make me wise, so that I may know the things you have taught my people, the lessons you have hidden in every leaf and rock. I seek strength, O Great Spirit, not to be superior to others but to be able to fight my greatest enemy, myself. Make me ever ready to come to you with clean hands and straight eyes so that when life fades as the fading sunset, my spirit may come to you without shame.

This beautiful prayer was written by Tom White Cloud, an Ojibway Indian, and carved in stone by members of the Akwesasne Mohawk Counselor Organization of Hogansburg, New York. It is placed at a roadside rest area in upstate New York to strengthen and inspire passersby. It offers encouragement for the journey at hand and hope and courage in the journey of life.

☾*

O JESUS, BE THE CANOE

Melanesian Prayer

O Jesus,
Be the canoe that holds me up in the sea of life;
Be the rudder that keeps me in the straight road;
Be the outrigger that supports me in times of temptation.
Let your Spirit be my sail that carries me through each day.
Keep my body strong, so I can paddle steadfastly on
in the voyage of life.

"O Jesus, Be the Canoe" is a gift from Melanesia, the largest and most diverse group of islands of Oceania, which lies west of Papua New Guinea. The prayer is used by members of the Pacific Conference of Churches, the ecumenical group of Pacific Island churches. The Conference promotes the development of a theology of the Pacific, sometimes called "coconut palm theology," which emphasizes the enormous riches those of different island cultures and traditions have to share with each other.

C*

CREATING GOD, YOUR FINGERS TRACE

Jeffery Rowthorn

Creating God, your fingers trace
the bold designs of farthest space;
let sun and moon and stars and light
and what lies hidden praise your might.

Sustaining God, your hands uphold
earth's mysteries known or yet untold;
let water's fragile blend with air,
enabling life, proclaim your care.

Redeeming God, your arms embrace
all now despised for creed or race;
let peace, descending like a dove,
make known on earth your healing love.

Indwelling God, your gospel claims
one family with a billion names;
let every life be touched by grace
until we praise you face to face.

This hymn, a contemporary paraphrase of Psalm 148, launched Jeffery Rowthorn's (born 1934) career as a hymn writer and won first place in a Hymn Society of America competition. According to Rowthorn, "I wrote the hymn to underline the continuous activity of God who did not once and for all create the world, but who is continuously, actively creating. I also wanted to underscore both the fragility and the beauty of the created order, which modern science has led us to appreciate more profoundly."

C*

ARCHITECT OF THE WORLDS

Free Church of Berkeley

Architect of the worlds,
you put man and woman in the garden to keep it.
Show us the true harmony between ourselves and the earth,
between green things and animals, air and water.
Give us the secrets of knowledge and will,
to restore all damage done to the planet
by our ignorance or malice,
and let all living things have the freedom
which is proper for them.

Readers old enough to have participated in the protest movements of the 1960s and early 1970s may feel a pang of nostalgia as they read "Architect of the Worlds" and the two other selections in this book from the Free Church of Berkeley. According to its founders, the Free Church was "committed by the Gospel of Love and the needs of the planet to the struggle for peace, justice, and environmental renewal."

☾*

COVERED with FROST FLOWERS

Zuñi Prayer

That our Earth Mother may wrap herself
In a fourfold robe of white meal;
That she may be covered with frost flowers;
That yonder on all the mossy mountains,
The forests may huddle together with the cold;
That their arms may be broken by the snow,
In order that the land may be thus,
I have made my prayer sticks into living beings.

The unidentified Zuñi poet creates an image of a frozen winter landscape covered with "frost flowers" and forests "huddled together with the cold." Could the breaking of the ice-heavy branches signify the breaking into awareness of insights that come to light in this bleakest ebb of the year?

☾*

O GOD, MAY I SPEAK...

Chiara Lubich

O God,

May I ever speak
    as though it were the last word that I can speak.

May I ever act
    as though it were the last action I can perform.

May I ever suffer
    as though it were the last pain I can offer.

May I ever pray
    as though it were for me on earth
    the last chance to speak to you. Amen.

In 1943, as bombs were falling over war-torn Europe, Chiara Lubich (born in 1920), a young Italian woman, founded a movement calling people to live simply in community, to pray together for peace, and to practice everyday spirituality in their jobs. It was called Focolare — a word meaning "hearth" in Italian — because of the warm gathering of people drawn together by the fire of their faith.

☾*

Chapter 3

POEMS

My heart is moved by all I cannot save; so much has been destroyed. I have cast my lot with those who age after age, perversely, with no extraordinary power, reconstitute the world.

— Adrienne Rich
The Dream of a Common Language

I AM THE WIND

Amergin

I am the wind which breathes upon the sea,
I am the wave of the ocean,
I am the murmur of the willows,
I am the ox of the seven combats,
I am the vulture upon the rocks,
I am the beam of the sun,
I am the fairest of plants,
I am the wild boar in valor,
I am the salmon in the water,
I am the lake in the plain,
I am a word of knowledge....
I am the God who created the fire....

"I Am the Wind" is thought to be the first poem ever composed in Ireland. It is attributed to Amergin, a prince who is said to have lived a hundred years before the birth of Christ. The Celts had an overpowering sense of the divine presence permeating every aspect of creation. Amergin articulates clearly the pantheistic animism that inspired the Celtic people of these emerald islands long before the coming of Christianity.

☾*

GOD OF ALL

Saint Patrick

Our God is the God of all...
the God of heaven and earth,
the God of sea, of river, of sun and moon and stars,
of the lofty mountains and the lowly valleys.
The God above heaven,
The God under heaven,
The God in heaven.
God dwells around heaven,
and earth and sea, and all that is part of them,
God inspires all,
God quickens all,
God dominates all,
God sustains all,
God lights the light of the sun.
God furnishes the light of light.

Saint Patrick (ca. 387–ca. 461), patron saint of Ireland, does not have a drop of Irish blood in him. An English youth, he was carried off as a slave to Ireland. It was there that he received a vision that he was to dedicate himself to the conversion of the Irish people to Christianity. Saint Patrick was a mystic with an overpowering sense of the presence of God intimately woven into every aspect of the natural world.

☾*

AFTON WATER

Robert Burns

Flow gently, sweet Afton, among thy green braes[1],
Flow gently, I'll sing thee a song in thy praise;
My Mary's asleep by the murmuring stream,
Flow gently, sweet Afton, disturb not her dream.

Thou stock-dove whose echo resounds through the glen,
Ye wild whistling blackbirds in yon thorny den,
Thou green-crested lapwing, thy screaming forbear,
I charge you disturb not my slumbering fair.

How lofty, sweet Afton, thy neighboring hills,
How marked with the courses of clear winding rills;
There daily I wander as noon rises high,
My flocks and my Mary's sweet cot[2] in my eye.

How pleasant thy banks and green valleys below,
Where wild in the woodlands the primroses blow;
There oft as mild evening weeps over the lea,
The sweet-scented birk[3] shades my Mary and me.

---

[1] hillsides
[2] cottage
[3] birch

Thy crystal stream, Afton, how lovely it glides,
And winds by the cot where my Mary resides;
How wanton thy waters her snowy feet lave,
As gathering sweet flowerets she stems thy clear wave.

Flow gently, sweet Afton, among they green braes,
Flow gently, sweet river, the theme of my lays;
My Mary's asleep by thy murmuring stream,
Flow gently, sweet Afton, disturb not her dream.

The "Heaven-taught plowman," Robert Burns (1759–1796), was a self-educated Scottish peasant-farmer. He loved life, nature, women, poetry, and music and amply indulged in all these tastes during his short life of thirty-seven years. The graceful "Afton Water" was written in the early spring of 1789 on the banks of the Afton River in southwestern Scotland.

☾*

NIGHT

William Blake

The sun descending in the west
The evening star does shine,
The birds are silent in their nest

And I must seek for mine.
The moon, like a flower
In heaven's high bower,
With silent delight
Sits and smiles on the night.

Farewell green fields and happy groves
Where flocks have took delight;
Where lambs have nibbled, silent moves
The feet of angels bright;
Unseen they pour their blessing
And joy without ceasing
On each bud and blossom
And each sleeping bosom.

They look in every thoughtless nest
Where birds are covered warm,
They visit caves of every beast
To keep them all from harm.
If they see any weeping
That should have been sleeping,
They pour sleep on their head
And sit down by their bed.

William Blake (1757–1825), a British lyric poet and painter, was one of the best exemplars of the first generation of romantics that included Wordsworth, Coleridge, and artists

Gainsborough and Turner. During the second half of nineteenth century, writers and artists were rediscovering the natural world, which they often personalized and glorified. In "Night," Blake presents a peaceable world watched over by angels who, unseen, "pour blessing and joy without ceasing."

☾*

FLOWER IN THE CRANNIED WALL

Alfred, Lord Tennyson

Flower in the crannied wall,
I pluck you out of the crannies,
I hold you here, root and all, in my hand,
Little flower — but *if* I could understand
What you are, root and all, and all in all,
I should know what God and man is.

Alfred, Lord Tennyson (1809–1892) has been called the "spokesman of the Victorian age." One of twelve children of a Church of England parson, Tennyson only ever wanted to be a poet and, in fact, his first volume of poems was published when he was just eighteen. His whole being was essentially conditioned by rural rather than urban life. He possessed the country person's awe at the splendor of something so small as a flower growing out of a crack in a wall.

☾*

AS THE BIRDS COME TO THE SPRING

Henry Wadsworth Longfellow

As the birds come to the spring,
　　We know not from where;
As the stars come at evening
　　From depths of the air;

As the rain comes from the cloud,
　　And the brook from the ground;
As suddenly, low or loud,
　　Out of silence a sound;

As the grape comes to the wine,
　　The fruit to the tree;
As the wind comes to the pine,
　　And the tide to the sea;

As come the white sails of ships;
　　O'er the ocean's verge;
As comes the smile to the lips,
　　The foam to the serve;

So come to the Poet his songs,
　　All hitherward blown

From the misty realm, that belongs
    to the vast Unknown.

Henry Wadsworth Longfellow (1807–1882) is the quintessential American poet. There are few of our grandparents who were not reared on at least a few of his famous poems — "Hiawatha," "The Courtship of Miles Standish," "The Wreck of the Hesperus," "The Village Blacksmith," or "Paul Revere's Ride." "As the Birds Come to the Spring" is excerpted from L'Envoi (the sending). Longfellow's poetry was also so admired abroad that shortly after his death he became the first American to be given a place in Poet's Corner at Westminster Abbey in London.

☾*

THE GREAT BLUE HERON

Author Unknown

Out of their loneliness for each other
two reeds, or maybe two shadows, lurch
forward and become suddenly a life
lifted from dawn or the rain. It is
the wilderness come back again, a lagoon
with our city reflected in its eye.
We live by faith in such presences.

It is a test for us, that thin
but real, undulating figure that promises,
"If you keep faith I will exist
at the edge, where your vision joins
the sunlight and the rain: heads in the light,
feet that go down in the mud where truth is."

This poem appears on a plaque at Portland City Hall because the great blue heron is the city bird of Portland, Oregon.

☪*

OH EARTH, WAIT FOR ME

Pablo Neruda

Return me, oh sun,
to my wild destiny,
rain of the ancient wood,
bring me back the aroma and the swords
that fall from the sky,
the solitary peace of pasture and rock,
the damp at the river margins,
the smell of the larch tree,

the wind alive like a heart
beating in the crowded restlessness
of the towering araucaria.

Earth, give me back your pure gifts,
the towers of silence, which rose
from the solemnity of their roots.
I want to go back to being what I have not been,
and learn to go back from such deeps
that amongst all natural things
I could live or not live; it does not matter
to be one stone more, the dark stone,
the pure stone which the river bears away.

The Chilean poet, diplomat, and politician Pablo Neruda (1904–1973) is considered one of the most original and prolific poets to write in the Spanish language in the twentieth century. His talent gained him the Nobel Prize for Literature in 1971. As much a man of compassion as a writer, this precocious son of a railway worker was an ardent lover of life and a champion of the rights of the oppressed and downtrodden.

☪*

SNOW IS FALLING

Boris Pasternak

Snow is falling, snow is falling:
Stretching to the window pane
Pale geraniums gaze out
Where the starflakes blow white rain.

Snow is falling, all's a flurry,
Everything wings off and flies:
Steps down in the shadowed staircase,
Corner where the crossroads rise.

Snow is falling, snow is falling —
Somehow, though, not flakes teem round
But heaven's arch, in ragged furs,
Is descending to the ground.

Looking like an old eccentric,
From the upper landing sly —
Creeping, playing hide-and-seek —
From its attic steals the sky.

Flow of life is not for waiting;
Eyelid's wink, Christmas is here:

Just a moment, time's brief passing,
Look around and it's New Year.

Snow is falling, faster, faster:
Stepping out in rhythmic feet,
Tempo same and same the drag,
Might not with the selfsame beat
Time itself flit by and pass?
Might not all the years come and go
Like all the words knit into a poem,
Like the falling of the snow?

Snow is falling, snow is falling,
Snow is falling, all's a flurry —
Whitened walker in a hurry,
Flowers covered with surprise,
Corners where the crossroads rise.

Boris Pasternak (1890–1960), the great Russian novelist, was first and foremost a poet. His first volume of poetry was published just before World War I and he appended twenty-five poems to Dr. Zhivago, *written in 1957. Pasternak lived through the immense hardships and upheavals of Russian society during the twentieth century. He was discredited and many of his manuscripts lost and confiscated, yet this humble poet never lost his sense of the wonder of God's creation nor the simple pleasure of watching the snow fall in the depths of a cold Russian winter.*

☾*

EVERY BEING IN THE UNIVERSE

Lao Tzu

Every being in the universe
Is an expression of God.
All life springs into existence,
unconscious,
perfect,
free,
taking on shapes,
letting circumstances
bring it to completion.

God gives birth to all things,
nourishes them,
maintains them,
cares for them,
comforts them,
protects them,
takes them back to herself,
creating without possessing,
acting without expecting,
guiding without interfering.

This is why the
love of God

is in the very nature of things,
in every being in the universe.

*Nothing is known about Lao Tzu (ca. 571 B.C.E.), whose name means "old philosopher,"
except that he left behind him a book of eighty-one chapters that for the last two thousand years
has been called* Tao Te Ching. *This modest little book bred Taoism, and deeply influenced
Buddhism; it led to Ch'an and Zen meditation and inspired Chinese poetry and landscape
painting. For centuries it was Asia's most read book, and it continues to serve as a guide for
persons in their search for the universal meaning of existence.*

☪*

IMAGINING THE DIVINE

Diane Ackerman

On cold days, the divine haunts
the exhalations of squirrels
whose breath hovers
starch-white as tiny souls.

Like the sky, heaven begins
at one's feet. Look down.

When the here and now
becomes the there and then,
the redwinged blackbird's rasp
sounds angelic, summer croons
pontifications of light,
and, my god, life fancies trees.

Because I believe we become
a neverthriving of dreams,
all our senses levelled,
I imagine the divine
drawing on of evening,
belted at the waist,
the divine cloud-slung stars
burning black holes
into the fabric of night,

I divine the lusty sun
in each aching-green leaf,
and revere the silver
ceremonies of the moon
cradled in its own arms.

Just imagine the divine
hilltops padded with trees,
the bone-wings of a river basin

hipped in daylilies, Canada goose chicks:
fluff-budgets that waddle.

Before my one and only
three-pound universe, I stand
in judgment, alone with the world,
so long as we both shall live,
or vanish when eyelids close.

Because life will have been all
my days, I imagine the divine
face of my loving dear,
who shares the harsh and softer fate-falls
inside these garden walls
where the divine agency of love
will have mattered in the end
more than faith, call, reward,
or a vein of panting stars.

Like the planet, we seemed
to be travelling through space
but were always in a holding pattern
between the earth and sky,
waiting to unbecome, plural once more.

The divine I imagine
speaks to me through pleats

of perfect taffeta in my study,
between the wingbeats of hummingbirds,
when love smiles humbly
at sunrise and in evening rain.

The contemporary poet, Diane Ackerman, imagines the divine speaking to her ". . . through pleats of perfect taffeta . . . , between the wingbeats of hummingbirds, when love smiles humbly at sunrise and in evening rain." Where and at what moments does the Creator God of heaven and earth speak to you and touch your life?

C*

FLOWING ALONG THE BORDER OF HEAVEN

Li Po

My friend bids farewell at the Yellow Crane House,
And heads down eastwards to Willow Valley
Amid the flowers and mists of March.
The lonely sail in the distance
Vanishes at last beyond the blue sky
And I can see only the river
Flowing along the border of heaven.

The relationship between poetry and painting is well illustrated by Li Po's (701–762) poem. Because of the intimate relationship between the two art forms, both of which speak to the innermost thoughts of the human soul, they are often combined on one scroll that contains a poem and a painting of the scene described by the poem.

☾*

EVERY PETAL, EVERY SPECK

Liu K'O-chuang

Every petal is light as the butterfly's raiment;
Every speck is blood-red and tiny.
If you say that God cares not for the flowers,
Consider the hundred kinds and the thousand varieties,
    skillfully fashioned.

At morn you see the tree tops luxuriant,
At eve you see the ranch-tops denuded.
If you say that God, in truth, cares for the flowers,
Consider the rain's drenching, and the wind's blast.

Liu K'O-chaung (1187–1269) was a highly respected poet of the Sung Dynasty. This poem expresses a comprehensive sense of God's presence in every aspect of creation, from the tiniest petal to the wind's mightiest blast.

☾*

IN THE SIXTH MONTH

Selected haiku from the works of Bashō

In the sixth month
Mount Arashi
    lays clouds on its summit.

❦

Harvest moon —
walking around the pond
    all night long.

❦

A petal shower
of mountain roses,
    and the sound of rapids.

❦

Coolness of the melons
flecked with mud
    in the morning dew.

❦

Winter solitude —
in a world of one color
    the sound of wind.

The hollyhocks
lean toward the sun
in May rain.

The dragonfly
can't quite land
on that blade of grass.

A field of cotton —
as if the moon
had flowered.

Bashō (1644–1694) believed that contemplating and writing about ordinary elements and actions around him would lead to the deepening of all life experience. He took his pen name, Bashō, from the luxuriant, broad-leafed banana tree his students gave him as a gift. The poet was born in western Japan; he studied Japanese and Chinese classics and went to Edo (now Tokyo) to learn poetry and Zen. By the age of thirty-four, Bashō had become the leader of a group of young poets at the center of the literary life of the capital. In his forties he embarked on a wandering life, staying at monasteries and country houses, writing as he went. Today Bashō is considered one of the world's all-time greatest lyric poets.

☾*

THE DAFFODILS

William Wordsworth

I wandered lonely as a cloud
That floats on high o'er vales and hills,
When all at once I saw a crowd,
A host of golden daffodils,
Beside the lake, beneath the trees
Fluttering and dancing in the breeze.

Continuous as the stars that shine
And twinkle on the milky way,
They stretched in never-ending line
Along the margin of a bay:
Ten thousand I saw at a glance
Tossing their heads in sprightly dance.

The waves beside them danced, but they
Out-did the sparkling waves in glee:
A poet could not but be gay
In such a jocund company!
I gazed — and gazed — but little thought
What wealth the show to me had brought:

But oft, when on my couch I lie
In vacant or in pensive mood,

They flash upon that inward eye,
Which is the bliss of solitude;
And then my heart with pleasure fills,
And dances with the daffodils.

William Wordsworth (1770–1850) is foremost of the great nature poets of England and "The Daffodils" is one of the best known of all such poems of the nineteenth century. His poetry is particularly noted for its descriptive power and its sense of wonder at the beauties of nature. He wrote in a direct, picturesque, and conversational manner, rejecting the formalism of eighteenth-century poets. Wordsworth spent most of his life in the English Lake District where daffodils still grow in great profusion at Dove Cottage, his little house at Grasmere.

☾*

SPRING SONG

Robert Browning

The year's at the spring
And day's at the morn;
Morning's at seven;
The hillside's dew-pearled;
The lark's on the wing;
The snail's on the thorn;

God's in his heaven —
All's right with the world.

"Spring Song" is taken from Robert Browning's well-known poem, "Pippa Passes." Browning (1812–1889), a poet of the romantic era, considered himself mainly a botanist, which would explain why many of his themes drawn from nature. The change of seasons is a universal poetic theme that transcends culture and time.

☪*

THE WAKING

Theodore Roethke

I wake to sleep, and take my waking slow.
I feel my fate in what I cannot fear.
I learn by going where I have to go.

We think by feeling. What is there to know?
I hear my being dance from ear to ear.
I wake to sleep, and take my waking slow.

Of those so close beside me, which are you?
God bless the Ground! I shall walk softly there,
And learn by going where I have to go.

Light takes the Tree; but who can tell us how?
The lowly worm climbs up a winding stair;
I wake to sleep, and take my waking slow.

Great Nature has another thing to do
To you and me; so take the lively air,
And, lovely, learn by going where to go.

This shaking keeps me steady. I should know.
What falls away is always. And is near,
I wake to sleep, and take my waking slow.
I learn by going where I have to go.

Theodore Roethke (1908–1963) was born in Saginaw, Michigan, and grew up in a wooded sanctuary. Roethke's was a troubled childhood and his entire life was an odyssey in search of himself. Throughout it, he found solace and order in growing things. His profound reverence for life is reflected in his nature poetry. "The Waking" traces the poet's long journey towards self-knowledge and fulfillment, through mental breakdowns and bereavements, and finally to love. It is included in this anthology because of the idea of walking softly on the sacred ground, and by doing so, learning where we ought to go.

☪*

IN HARDWOOD GROVES

Robert Frost

The same leaves over and over again!
They fall from giving shade above
To make one texture of faded brown
And fit the earth like a leather glove.

Before the leaves can mount again
To fill the trees with another shade,
They must go down past things coming up,
They must go down into the dark decayed.

They *must* be pierced by flowers and put
Beneath the feet of dancing flowers.
However it is in some other world
I know that this is the way in ours.

"In Hardwood Groves" begins with a simple idea, a straightforward fact — "The same leaves fall over and over again!" Period. Then, unwittingly and unprepared, the reader is led by the artful poet to a consideration of death and resurrection, of life descending into decay then giving birth to life "pierced by flowers."

☾*

BEES

Lo Yin

Down in the plain, and up on the mountaintop,
All nature's boundless glory is their prey.
But when they have sipped from a hundred flowers
    and made honey,
For whom is this toil, for whom this nectar?

Lo Yin (833–909), a poet of T'ang Dynasty, was a native of Hangchow, China. He wrote simple and popular yet provocative poetry. In "Bees" the poet begs the question as to who the works of creation are for. What purpose do they serve? Is the toil of the bee for its own glory? What place does the bee have in the wider scheme of nature? The humble bee is an insect of great power. Its sting has been known to kill a giant; its honey delights the palates of princes.

☾*

ENCHANTMENTS OF THE RIVER

Paulo Gabriel

You need to sail naked
through what is left of the forest
to discover what the earth was in the beginning.

And then penetrate, deeply moved,
through the spaces of light that the river offers
where the forest and the water balance,
wisely governed by the birds.

For it is only here where the earth
is not yet desecrated
that the ugly fear of death
spawned by human beings, does not reign.

On the beach, the turtle lays its eggs,
contemplated by the stork;
and on the sand the alligator rests,
serious, like a general in uniform.

The tortoise spies from the woods;
wild ducks and toucans drink the morning breeze
while a band of yellow butterflies announce
that the world is fragile, like a dance.

Along the riverbank, searching for water,
roots reveal the direction of life.
It seems that goodness passed through the world
before consciousness was perverted.

Today I don't want to meet anyone,
just stay by the river forever,

to judge without hurting it,
the true dimension of the earth.

Paulo Gabriel, a popular singer in Brazil, has been described as a "builder of fantasies, dreamer of a new world, a mason of utopias." This poem was taken from "And God Saw That It Was Good...", a book of liturgies used during an international consultation sponsored by the World Council of Churches in São Paulo in June, 1988, entitled God, People and Nature: One Community.

C*

THE CHILL SNOW

Yeh Pao-sung

The chill snow is heaped against the sunlit window;
I burn my incense, and rejoice to comprehend
    the Way of Buddha.
Out in the bamboos a bluecap calls,
And the breeze sways a snow-covered twig.

Yeh Pao-sung was a Chinese landscape poet of the Ch'ing Dynasty. A Buddhist, he used a simple setting, probably his home, as a location for meditation. He was fully awake (in the

Buddhist sense of being awake) to the cold snow outside his window and the call of the bird from the bamboo grove beyond. He concentrated his attention on just one snow-covered twig and through it sought to "comprehend the Way of the Buddha."

☾*

GREEN LEAVES, WHITE WATER

Selected Haiku from the Works of the Poet Buson

Green leaves,
white water,
the barley yellowing.

❧

The spring sea rising
and falling, rising
and falling all day.

❧

Ploughing the land —
not even a bird singing
in the mountain's shadow.

❧

Not quite dark yet
and the stars shining
            above the withered fields.

In the summer rain
the path
            has disappeared.

Wild geese returning
on a night when in every rice field
            the mood is clouding.

By moonlight
the blossoming plum
            is a tree in winter.

Not a leaf stirring;
frightening,
            the summer grove.

The end of spring

      lingers

           in the cherry blossoms.

Buson (1716–1783) was not only a great poet but also a distinguished painter of his day. He was born near Osaka, the son of a wealthy farmer. When he was twenty he went to Edo to study poetry and painting, especially the Chinese masters of the T'ang school. Later he wandered through the north country of Japan, retracing Bashō's journeys. Buson's writing is prized for its clarity and sense of the aliveness of things and their presence.

FRIENDS WE SHALL BECOME

Geoffrey Duncan

You saw the sun rising from the sea,
I saw the moon rising from the mountains.
We argued for a long time.
You say it's summer,
I say it's winter.
We argued for a long time.
Then you visited me in the south,

Then I visited you in the north.
We saw new worlds.
You saw the black forests in my country,
I saw the eternal snows on your mountain peaks.
We agreed that the beauty of white is in its clear brightness,
And the beauty of black is in its mysterious darkness.
Sharing — face to face — friends we shall become,
And in peace we shall create, you and me.

This poem was used as a prayer at a worldwide gathering of Anglican bishops and their spouses at Saint Paul's Cathedral in London, in July, 1998, during a service called a "Feast of the Kingdom."

☾*

THE EAGLE

Alfred, Lord Tennyson

He clasps the crag with crooked hands;
Close to the sun in lonely lands,
Ringed with the azure world, he stands.

The wrinkled sea beneath him crawls;
He watches from his mountain walls,
And like a thunderbolt he falls.

With "The Eagle," composed in 1851, Tennyson invites us to close our eyes and imagine a vast windswept land, to hear the howling of the wind against the barren branches, and there to picture the majestic eagle circling the azure sky, then diving "like a thunderbolt."

☾*

NEW FEET WITHIN MY GARDEN GO

Emily Dickinson

New feet within my garden go —
New fingers stir the sod.
A troubadour upon the elm
Betrays the solitude.

New children play upon the green —
New weary sleep below,
And still the pensive spring returns,
And still the punctual snow.

Only two of Emily Dickinson's (1830–1886) now famous poems were published during her lifetime. The rest of the fifteen hundred poems were discovered after her death, mostly written on scraps of paper and scattered about in drawers and boxes. By the time she was thirty-five, the world of this shy, reclusive poet had shrunk to her father's house and garden where this poem was written.

☾*

A PRAYER IN SPRING

Robert Frost

Oh, give us pleasure in the flower today;
And give us not to think so far away
As the uncertain harvest; keep us here
All simply in the springing of the year.

Oh, give us pleasure in the orchard white,
Like nothing else by day, like ghosts by night;
And make us happy in the happy bees,
The swarm dilating round the perfect trees.

And make us happy in the darting bird
That suddenly above the bee is heard,
the meteor that thrusts in with the needle bill,
And off a blossom in mid air stands still.

For this is love and nothing else is love,
The which is reserved for God above
To sanctify to what far ends He will,
But which it only needs we fulfill.

Robert Frost would never have called himself religious, yet here is a straightforward prayer
of thanksgiving for the beauty of a fragrant orchard of flowers (probably apple blossoms),

"happy bees," and a "darting bird." In the poet's world, vision extends imagination; to sight is added insight; and love, touching the depths of eternity, overrides all.

☾*

THE MAPLE GROVE

Yüan Hao-wen

By the distant rill the maple grove looks scattered;
By the deep mountain the lane of bamboos looks peaceful;
The thin mist swallows up the departing birds;
The thin mist of the sinking sun companions the homing cattle.

Yüan Hao-wen (1190–1257) was the outstanding literary figure of his period (Sung Dynasty) in China. He was highly regarded as a poet and prose writer. "The Maple Grove" is part of a series of poems on the theme of mountain life.

☾*

QUESTION AND ANSWER
AMONG THE MOUNTAINS

Li Po

You ask me why I dwell in the green mountain;
I smile and make no reply for my heart is free to care.
As the peach blossom flows down the stream and is gone
    into the unknown,
I have a world apart that is among no one.

Li Po (701–762) is regarded as the greatest poet of the Chinese T'ang Dynasty. He left his home in Szechwan about 720 and for twenty years wandered from place to place only occasionally working. For a short period (742–744) he was a court poet at the provincial capital of Ch'ang-an, but preferred his carefree nomadic life.

C*

A SINGLE PLUM TREE

Chu Tun-ju

By the ancient rill there is a single plum tree
That refuses to be imprisoned in garden or park.
Far away in the mountain depth it fears not the cold,

As though at hide-and-seek with Spring.
My inmost thoughts, who can know them?
Ties of friendship are hard to make.
Alone in my romance, alone in my fragrance,
The moon comes to look for me.

Chu Tun-ju (ca. 1080–ca. 1175) was a reclusive, wandering poet of the Sung Period. As "A Single Plum Tree" illustrates, Chu Tun-ju was an intense observer of nature and like so many others throughout every age, he took comfort from life's disappointments and sorrows in the natural world. Friendship and romance might elude one but never the moon. It may wax and wane but it is always there.

☾*

IN THIS WORLD

Selected Haiku from the Works of Issa

In this world —
we walk on the roof of hell,
gazing at flowers.

🦋

A good world —
the dewdrops fall
by ones, by twos.

Crescent moon —
bent to the shape
of the cold.

The cuckoo sings
to me, to the mountain,
to me, to the mountain.

New Year's morning:
the ducks on the pond
quack and quack.

The evening clears —
on the pale sky
row on row of autumn mountains.

Insects on a bough
floating downriver,
still singing.

Issa (1763–1827) was a farmer's son born in a small mountain village in central Japan. Like Bashō and Buson, he went to Edo to study poetry and three years later became the master of his poetry center. Issa studied Buddhism and became a monk, then he began an itin-erant life. Issa wrote hundreds of poems and he was particularly fond of the smallest creatures —flies, fleas, crickets, even bedbugs and lice.

☽*

TONIGHT THE WINDS BEGIN TO RISE

Alfred, Lord Tennyson

Tonight the winds begin to rise
And roar from yonder dropping day;
The last red leaf is whirled away,
The rooks are blown about the skies.

The forest cracked, the waters curled,
The cattle huddled on the lea;
And wildly dashed on tower and tree
The sunbeam strikes along the world.

This poem comes from In Memoriam A. H. H., *a long series of verses written over a period of seventeen years in honor of Tennyson's closest friend, Arthur Hallam, who died suddenly in Italy at the age of twenty-two. The entire work traces Tennyson's transition from utter despair at the loss of his friend to acceptance and finally to a joyful embracing of the future. This poem established Tennyson's reputation as a poet and in the year of its publica-tion in 1850, he succeeded Wordsworth as Poet Laureate of England.*

☾*

COME IN

Robert Frost

As I came through to the edge of the woods,
Thrush music — hark!
Now if it was dusk outside,
Inside it was dark.

Too dark in the woods for a bird
By slight of wing
To better its perch for the night,
Though it still could sing.

The last of the light of the sun
That had died in the west
Still lived for one song more
In a thrush's breast.

Far in the pillared dark
Thrush music went —

Almost like a call to come in
To the dark and lament.

But no, I was out for stars:
I would not come in.
I meant not even if asked,
And I hadn't been.

In 1912, Robert Frost (1874–1963) was fighting the discouragement of being almost forty without having published a single volume. This unknown writer sold his farm in Derry, New Hampshire, and set out for England — a sheaf of poems in hand — where he'd heard the prospects for new talent were better. Within a year, A Boy's Will *was published, followed quickly by* North of Boston. *When the latter book was taken home by the Boston poet Amy Lowell, it became an immediate best-seller. In 1915 Frost returned to the United States to find himself suddenly and unexpectedly famous.*

☾*

EARTH SONG

Don DiVecchio

We are the earth, clay soft, reddish iron
    ashen gray, pungent clear soil.
We are of earth, sequoia, redwood, rooted.
In corn and wheat, with the bones of our ancestors.
We are of salt, ocean and pitched pine
The sun's heat moves within us —
We belong to each other, move together
Need each other.
We are of wind and fire
Our blood is rain
Our hearts are rivers
We are of Earth.
Our beauty is rooted in our past and present
    in our humanness.
We are the poor, the hungry, the war ravished,
We are the innocent and battered,
Our beauty is in the struggle to find ourselves,
We claim love lost
for all people.
We are roots to soil,
Trees to water, we are a part of each other.
Hurting one person hurts us all

Denying one being equality
Denies us all.
We are of Earth.

Contemporary poet Don DiVecchio is also a playwright, lecturer, and social activist. He says, "the poem, 'Earth Song,' is about our universal connectedness to the Earth, each other, and all living beings."

C*

FOR TWO THOUSAND MILES

Kao K'O-kung

For two thousand miles the land is fair
    with hills and streams,
Uncounted cherry-apples fringe the high road.
The wind bears along the fallen petals to mingle
    with the passing horses;
Those winds of spring, how they surpass even
    the wayfarers in their bustle.

Kao K'O-kung (1248–1310), a poet of the Yüan Dynasty, is best known as a land-scape pen and ink painter, and perhaps he painted a paysage to accompany this poem. This supposition seems likely since "For Two Thousand Miles" contains classic elements of Chinese landscape painting: hills, streams, a cherry tree, and the suggestion of travelers hunkering down in the spring winds.

☾*

ASK THE ANIMALS

Job 12:7–10

Ask the animals,
    and they will teach you.

Ask the birds of the air,
    and they will tell you.

Ask the plants of the earth,
    and they will inform you.

Ask the fish of the sea,
    and they will declare to you.

Who among you does not know
    that the hand of God has done all this?

In God's hand is the life of every living thing,
    and the breath of every human being.

In this reading from the Hebrew Scriptures, the humble man, Job, sees the natural world as the great classroom of life and wisdom. Animals, birds, plants and fish all have something to teach human beings.

☾*

A QUIET TEMPLE THICK SET WITH FLOWERS

Selected Lines and Stanzas by Li Po

A quiet temple thick set with flowers;
A sequestered lake hidden in the fine bamboos.

What a lovely patch of green!
I know it's grass on the other side of the lake.
What a glorious stretch of crimson!
I see it's clouds beyond the eastern sea.

A tortoise leaves a watery patch behind it,
As it sails slowly through the duckweeds.

Kingfishers are chirping on a clothesline.
A dragonfly rests motionless on the silken cord of a fishing rod.

Entering into the peach blossoms,
Redness grows soft and tender.
Returning to the willow leaves,
Greenness becomes fresh and new.

The dark ravine oozes with the music of silence.
The bright moonlight is being sifted through the thick foliage.

A tiny rivulet trickles like a hidden thread through a flower path.
Spring stars girdle my grass hut like a necklace of pearls.

The emeraldine fine bamboos, in the gentle caress of the wind,
The red water lilies, bathed in the rain,
Send forth whiff after whiff of invisible incense.

Countless dragonflies are darting up and down in a group.
A pair of wild ducks float and dive together.

White sandy beaches and emerald bamboos
Embrace the river village in eventide.
The wooden door of my humble house
Seems to hold a hearty tete-a-tete with the new moon.

The autumn water is clear and fathomless.
It cleanses and refreshes the heart of the lonely traveler.

The peach blossoms and pear blossoms
Follow closely upon one another's heels to the ground.
The yellow birds and white birds
Sometimes mingle together in their flight.

The birds are whiter for the blue of the river;
The flowers almost burn on the green hills.

Darting upwards, a bee gets tangled in a falling catkin.
Forming a line, the ants are crawling up to a withered pear.

A gentle shower, and the little fish come to the surface;
The waters being deep, the fish are extremely happy.

The maples and orange trees,
Are playing for us a wonderful orchestra of colors!
The evening sun is smoking the fine grass.
The luminous river is sparkling through the screen.

The forest being thick, the birds feel right at home.
A little breeze, and the swallows are darting with slanting wings.

In the depth of the night the temple strikes me with a sudden awe.
The tinkling of the golden bells by the wind brings silence to the fore.

Blackness has enveloped the courtyard with all its spring colors.
Dark fragrance is haunting this stainless spot on earth.

The nice rain knows its season,
It is born of Spring.
It follows the wind secretly into the night,
And showers its blessings, silently, softly, upon everything.

The works of the great wandering poet of the T'ang Dynasty, Li Po (701–762), transmit a feeling of intimacy that leaps across centuries and cultures. The reader is not outside the poetry but swept up in the beauty described, finding new strength and happiness by identifying with its richness. When we are successful in making this identification, we will become like the gentle rain that "showers its blessings, silently, softly, upon everything."

☾*

WHAT A WONDERFUL WORLD

William Blake

To see a World in a Grain of Sand
and a Heaven in a Wild Flower,
hold Infinity in the palm of your hand
and Eternity in an hour.

When British poet William Blake was a child he had a vision in which he saw God look-ing at him through the window. The vision carried his eye beyond the window to a tree outside; the tree was full of angels. This vision never left him and Blake had many more throughout his life. He trusted his visions as bearers of truth and they became the source of his inspiration. Blake claimed that he first painted his visions and later wrote down words to accompany the paintings that had been dictated to him by God. "I copy imagination," he said. "I write when commanded by the spirits."

☾*

LAMENTATION OF THE ROCKS

Robert O'Rourke

Long ago nature's music played along
    the slopes of our sacred Chuska Mountains;
        their bright melodies lingered deep in the valleys.
My people, the Dineh, took solace in
    wind whispers,
        coyote songs,
            the silence of rocks and
                high-soaring eagles.
Today I return to this place where my ancestors
    gathered medicine herbs.
I stop to listen for the old melodies

running softly through the trees,
for the beating heart of Mother Earth,
the rhythm of sparkling waters.
The sonorous sounds are no more!
What remain are
lamentations of blasted boulders,
clanking of chain saws,
crashing trees,
rocks crumbling into dust.
My spirit yearns for the long-ago, lost harmonies —
the musing of insects,
rustle of leaves,
the voice of the hawk.
Stooping down, I choose one tormented rock;
holding it gently toward the sky;
together we pray to the GOD-OF-ALL-THINGS
for the return of earth song,
the murmur of grass,
butterfly wings and
the gentle silence of rocks
at peace.

Robert O'Rourke is a poet, wood-carver, and environmental activist living in Colorado. This modern day Saint Francis says of this poem: "My poem was written during a trip to the

Navajo Nation with my son, David. We crossed the Chuska Mountains on a rough, rugged road before we came to a place called Canyon de Chelly. All along the route trees were bull-dozed, rocks dynamited, the earth broken and scarred. It seemed to me that even the rocks cried out in pain. Wildlife must have been panicked by the blasting and desolation of their homes and habitat. It was enough to make us depressed and heart-broken."

C*

LINES WRITTEN IN EARLY SPRING

William Wordsworth

I heard a thousand blended notes,
While in a grove I sat reclined,
In that sweet mood when pleasant thoughts
Bring sad thoughts to mind.

To her fair works did Nature link
The human soul that through me ran;
And much it grieved my heart to think
What man has made of man.

Through primrose tufts, in that green bower,
The periwinkle trailed its wreaths;

And 'tis my faith that every flower
Enjoys the air it breathes.

The birds around me hopped and played,
Their thoughts cannot measure —
But the least motion which they made,
It seemed a thrill of pleasure.

The budding twigs spread out their fan,
To catch the breezy air;
And I must think, do all I can,
That there was pleasure there.

If this belief from heaven be sent
If such be Nature's holy plan,
Have I not reason to lament
What man has made of man?

The natural world provided not only Wordsworth's inspiration but also his comfort when he was low in spirits. This poem was written in 1798 following a cold and depressing winter spent in Germany. He was desperately homesick for his beloved Lake District and the sound of "a thousand blended notes" reinforced Wordsworth's nostalgia for his homeland.

C*

THE LITTLE PEACH TREES

Tai Fu-ku

The little peach trees, ownerless, blossom untended;
Above the waste of misty grass the ravens home for the night.
Here and there broken walls encircle ancient wells;
Erstwhile, each of these was someone's habitation.

 Tai Fu-ku was born in 1167; he lived to be more than eighty and was considered one of the better poets of the Southern Sung Period (1127–1279). He was masterful in his ability to capture a moment's vision in just four lines. Like Tai Fu-ku, most of us have come across ancient foundations, long overgrown with trees and vines, and wondered who might have lived there and why they departed.

☽*

CAPE ANN

T. S. Eliot

O quick quick quick, quick hear the song sparrow,
Swamp sparrow, fox sparrow, vesper sparrow
At dawn and dusk. Follow the dance
Of the goldfinch at noon. Leave to chance

The Blackburnian warbler, the shy one. Hail
With shrill whistle the note of the quail, the bobwhite
Dodging by baybush. Follow the feet
Of the walker, the water thrush. Follow the flight
Of the dancing arrow, the purple martin. Greet
In silence the bullbat. All are delectable. Sweet sweet sweet
But resign this land at the end, resign it
To its true owner, the tough one, the sea gull.
The palaver is finished.

Born in St. Louis, Thomas Stearns Eliot (1888–1965) went to England to begin his literary career as poet, playwright, and essayist. His early poetry is mostly concerned with the decay of the modern Western world. Having later experienced a religious conversion, the poet explored religious themes and the relationship between time and eternity. "Cape Ann" has no such lofty purpose! This poem is a description of the birds of Cape Ann, the northeasterly maritime region of Massachusetts. It concludes with the truth, well-known by anyone living by the sea — the noisy seagull is the captain of the coast.

☾*

LIGHT

Hyonsung Kim

All things of beauty on earth
Dwell under your roof.
You call them by names.
You shape their faces.
You open the gate to all creation.
When darkness comes to carry off our old shadows
You replace them with new ones drawn from tomorrow.
The bright hope in my heart is a jewel
Crystallized in your flames.

But it is not to be set in one hue.
Or shine in a small box.
You are sufficient.
You are perfect wherever you are.
When powerful your splendor overflows
My eyes, your little heaven.
Kind and passionate in my bosom,
In glory and beauty beyond,
More durable and brilliant in the distance,
Still warm and tender out of death's chill touch,
Whose life is that you are burning?
You are next to God.

Hyonsung Kim (1913–1976) was born in North Korea and his literary career began while he was a university student. Kim's work has evolved over three distinct periods. In his early years he was mainly concerned with the physical world (morning, dawn, trees, and the like). This stage was followed by his search for an inner world. In his final period, Kim's prevailing theme was loneliness as an essential part of human existence.

☾*

EARTH SONG

Ralph Waldo Emerson

Hear what the Earth says —

"Mine and yours;
Mine, not yours.
Earth endures;
Stars abide —
Shine down in the old sea;
Old are the shores;
But where are old men?
I who have seen so much,
Such have I never seen.

"The lawyer's deed
Ran sure,
In tail,
To them, and to their heirs
Who shall succeed,
Without fail,
Forevermore.

"Here is the land,
Shaggy with wood,
With its old valley,
Mound and flood.
But the heritors? —
Fled like the flood's foam.
The lawyer, and the laws,
And the kingdom,
Clean swept herefrom.

"They called me theirs,
Who so controlled me;
Yet every one
Wished to stay, and is gone.
How am I theirs,
If they cannot hold me,
But I hold them?"

"Earth Song" is the coda of Ralph Waldo Emerson's poem, "Hamatreya." In the body of the poem, he cites the names of the various landowners who "walked about his farm saying 'Tis mine, my children's and my name's.'" In "Earth Song," Emerson imagines what, if she had words, Mother Earth would say of such arrogance. They are all now lying in their graves while, according to Emerson, "Earth laughs in flowers [at] her boastful boys."

☪*

NOW FADES THE LAST LONG STREAK OF SNOW

Alfred, Lord Tennyson

Now fades the last long streak of snow,
Now burgeons every maze of quick
About the flowering squares[1] and thick
By ashen roots the violets blow.

Now rings the woodland loud and long,
The distance takes a lovelier hue,
And drowned in yonder living blue
The lark becomes a sightless song.

[1.] fields

Now dance the lights on lawn and lea,
The flocks are whiter down the vale,
And milkier every milky sail
On winding stream or distant sea;

Where now the seamew pipes, or dives
In yonder greening gleam, and fly
The happy birds, that change their sky
To build and brood, that live their lives

From land to land, and in my breast
Spring wakens too, and my regret
Becomes an April violet,
And buds and blossoms like the rest.

The short days of winter can darken the human spirit just as surely as they darken the iron sky. And delightful as it may be to watch a field fill up with snow, so there are few of us who regret winter's passing into spring. With the fading of the "last long streaks of snow," the dark moods of winter days soon become like April violets — new life awakening into flowers and blossoms.

C*

JOURNEY AT DAWN

Lin Shao-chan

A glow ushers in the dawn while the moon is still bright;
Over the sparse trees hang some fading stars.
On the hill-paths people are few;
In the depth of the blue wisteria,
Singing birds make two or three notes.

Petals of frost, heavy on my fur coat, strike chill,
But my heart is light as my horse's hoofs.
Ten miles of green mountain,
one stream of flowing water —
All add to the inspiration.

Although nothing is known about him, Chinese poet Lin Shao-chan probably lived in the late eleventh or twelfth century. Buddhism provided the spiritual basis for much of Chinese landscape poetry of which this poem is a fine example. Clearly evident is the influence of Buddhism with its concentration on a single bird's song and a few petals of frost.

C*

THE WATERFALL

Zhang Jiuling

Out of the mists and the clouds with a leap
    and a shuddering cry
The waterfall, red with the blood of the earth,
    crashes to death with a sigh,
Down past the shivering trees to the rocks
    where its waters die
To arise in a vapor of ghostly forms
    seeking again the sky.
They weave from the threads of the sun
    a rainbow of tremulous light
While the sound of their dying sighs is
    the voice of a storm in its might.
The mountains in beauty dressed
    stand awed by that magical sight
Of the wedding of heaven and earth
    in a waterfall's headlong flight.

The contemplation of this clear poem by T'ang Dynasty poet Zhang Jiuling (673–740) takes us right to the waterfall. It is as if we were there sitting alongside the poet. We can see the waterfall in our mind's eye. It is the springtime of the year and the stream is swollen with snowmelt. We see the rushing wild torrent, carrying red soil and stones in its wake, crashing on the boulders below. We see the mist rise up and in a sudden shaft of light a rainbow is revealed. For just a moment, heaven and earth are meeting in a flash of cosmic beauty.

☾*

I BELIEVE A LEAF OF GRASS...

Walt Whitman

I believe a leaf of grass is no less than the journeywork of the stars,
And the pismire is equally perfect, and a grain of sand,
     and the egg of the wren,
And the tree toad is a chef-d'oeuvre for the highest,
And the running blackberry would adorn the parlors of heaven,
And the narrowest hinge in my hand puts to scorn all machinery,
And the cow crunching with depressed head surpasses any statue,
And a mouse is miracle enough to stagger sextillions of infidels.
I find I incorporate gneiss, coal, long-threaded moss, fruits,
     grains, succulent roots,
And am stuccoed with quadrupeds and birds all over,
And have distanced what is behind me for good reasons,
But call anything back again when I desire it.
In vain the plutonic rocks send their old heat against my approach,
In vain the mastodon retreats beneath its own powdered,
In vain objects stand leagues off and assume manifold shapes,

In vain the ocean settling in hollows and the great monsters lying low,
In vain the buzzard houses herself with the sky,
In vain the snake slides through the creepers and logs,
In vain the elk takes to the inner passes of the woods,
In vain the razor-billed auk sails far north to Labrador,
I follow quickly, I ascend to the nest in the fissure of the cliff.

I think I could turn and live with animals, they are so placid
    and self-contained,
I stand and look at them long and long.
They do not sweat and whine about their condition,
They do not lie awake in the dark and weep for their sins,
They do not make me sick discussing their duty to God,
Not one is dissatisfied, not one is demented with the
    mania of owning things,
Not one kneels to one another, nor to this kind that lived thousands
    of years ago,
Not one is respectable or unhappy over the whole earth.
So they show their relations to me and I accept them,
They bring me tokens of myself....

"I Believe a Leaf of Grass" is an extract from a sweeping fifty-two stanza poem enti-tled "Song of Myself." Walt Whitman (1819–1892) is at one and the same time both irrev-erent and refreshing. Although he was never considered a poet of nature, this excerpt illustrates Whitman's sharp powers of observation and his appreciation of the natural world. Leaves of

Grass, *published in 1855, won Emerson's acclaim and almost immediately established*
Whitman's reputation as a writer.

C*

MOMENTS OF RISING MIST

Poets of the Sung Dynasty

You look but cannot reach,
You walk, the road goes twisting.
A path appears on the wood tip;
A thousand cliffs are visible beneath the clouds.
Fog and mist gleamed, now it is dark again.
The last glow lingers on the peak's tip.

❧

Waterfall echoes amidst the spring cliff,
Night is deep, the mountain is already quiet.
Bright moon washes the pine forest,
All the peaks are the same tint.

❧

Summer rain makes the forest muddy;
Slanting sunbeams reflect again and again.
Pure green, no wind ruffles it;
Let the spring grass smile!

Thousands of ridges stab at the clouds;
One glance is not enough.
Frontal ranges and the distant peaks,
Purplish blue, deep and light.

Enter the path and view the stone gate,
A vague green amidst the deep cloudy sky.
Clouds appear between the smooth stone steps,
Old trees and cold heavenly breeze.
Look at the last sun-glow; listen to the mountain cicadas.

These poems were written by Chinese landscape poets of the Sung Dynasty (960–1279).
The Sung period was one of the weakest politically but culturally one of the most splendid in
Chinese history. Both painting and poetry flourished, and many of the great painters of the age

were also poets. They believed that to know the place of human beings in the totality of the universe was the height of wisdom.

☾*

NOTHING GOLD CAN STAY

Robert Frost

Nature's first green is gold,
Her hardest hue to hold.
Her early leaf's a flower;
But only so an hour.
Then leaf subsides to leaf.
So Eden sank to grief,
So dawn goes down to day.
Nothing gold can stay.

An enduring poem is one that stays alive because it is rooted in mortal things and immortal emotions. Robert Frost said that a poem that truly satisfies will begin with "a lump in the throat, a homesickness, or a lovesickness. It is a reaching out toward expression; an effort to find fulfillment. A complete poem is one where an emotion has found its thought, and the thought has found the words." This is such a poem.

☾*

TEN THOUSAND THINGS RESPOND to SPRING SUN

Ou-yang Hsiu

Spring days are quiet, growing longer.
Fragrant wind enters the heart of the flowers;
Flowering branches at midday bob up and down.
Back and forth the bee picks among the blossoms;
his comb is not yet filled with clear honey.
Spring nights are most beautiful now;
Fallen petals one by one swirl through the air.
Yellow butterflies, nothing else to do,
Fly here and there to help them in their hurry.
Singing birds change their tune from time to time,
New notes skillfully blown from their flutes.
Spider webs are the idlest of all,
Their sunny light dangling a hundred feet.
The Heavenly Craftsman tends to creation's changes;
The ten thousand things respond to spring sun.

Ou-yang Hsiu (1007–1072, Sung Dynasty) was both a poet and a politician. As a Confucian master, he believed in the practical application of Confucianism to politics. As a poet he exhibits a directness and simplicity combined with great fluency. He was the acknowledged leader of the literary world of his generation.

C*

THE FIRST SNOW OF THE YEAR

Haiku from Four Japanese Poets

The first snow of the year,
On the bridge
    They are making.

                     — *Bashō*

The first snow;
Beyond the sea,
    What mountains are they?

                     — *Shiki*

There is neither heaven nor earth,
Only snow
    Falling incessantly.

                     — *Hashin*

Fields and mountains —
The snow has taken them all,
    Nothing remains.

                     — *Joso*

It was a universally held belief in Japan that literature came into being at the time the universe was created. Robert H. Blyth, translator of "The First Snow of the Year," first introduced haiku to English-speaking readers. He described this style of poetry as "the expression of a moment of vision into the nature of the world, the world of nature." He wrote that a haiku is "a record of a moment of emotion in which human nature is somehow linked to all nature."

☾*

SOUND

Kijo Song

I must go to the mountains
to hear
the sound of a brook
that's been breathing, ambushed,
under snow all winter
the sound of snow melting and ice defreezing
the sound of the spring opening
a breath crawling on the earth

The sound of trees growing
the sound of grass growing
the sound of flowers opening bud
the sound of sunlight getting wedged in the rocks

I must go to the mountains
to hear
the sound and the sound.

Traditional Korean poetry is influenced by the writings of the Chinese landscape poets as is evident in this contemporary poem by Kijo Song, born in 1932.

☪*

LOOKING FOR A SUNSET BIRD IN WINTER

Robert Frost

The west was getting out of gold,
The breath of air had died of cold,
When shoeing home across the white,
I thought I saw a bird alight.

In summer when I passed the place
I has to stop and lift my face;
A bird with an angelic gift
Was singing in it sweet and swift.

No bird was singing in it now.
A single leaf was on a bough,

And that was all there was to see
In going twice around the tree.

From my advantage on a hill
I judged that such a crystal chill
Was only adding frost to snow
As gilt to gold that wouldn't show.

A brush had left a crooked stroke
Of what was either cloud of smoke
From north to south across the blue
A piercing little star was through.

    While Robert Frost did not consider himself a "nature poet," the natural world was typically the focus of his poetic imagination. Human encounters with the earth became his means of illuminating metaphors for the larger aspects of the human condition. This is illustrated in "Looking for a Sunset Bird in Winter," which is about a bird who is not only unheard but unseen.

C*

THE FAR ECHOES OF THE TIDES

Tu Hsün-hê

I sit and watch
The flower-like moon
And the sparkling stars
Fade from the sky.
The shadows of the mountains
And the far echoes of the tides.

Tu Hsün-hê (late ninth century) was a poet of the late T'ang era. "The Far Reaches of the Tides" illustrates the classical Chinese poet's way of trapping a moment's vision within just a few lines. There is room between the artfully applied words for the reader to fill in the spaces and become part of this evening landscape. It is as if we were sitting quietly beside the poet watching "the flower-like moon and the sparkling stars fade from the sky."

☽*

SOMETHING GREATER THAN HEAVEN

Seuk Ho

Who calls me
that I go into barren emptiness
only to find a wind in the hollow corner
burrowing into the earholes of dandelions?

Who calls me
that I stand on the grass
where the crescent moon is moored while
I hear the dews dropping down
captured in the starry field all night long?

Who calls me
that when I feel the rail of dusking twilight
I hear the skeletons of leaves fallen last year
undulate their waists for a crawl?

Who calls me
that I cannot hear a sound
greater than the bell-sound when I come close to the hill
where the bell sounds?

Who calls me
as I go farther into emptiness

I find something greater emptied
something greater than heaven emptied —

Seuk Ho (born 1934) first made his name as a young poet living in Taiwan writing in Chinese in the 1960s. He began writing in Korean in 1969. Ho's themes are taken from nature. Here, he asks the universal question — Who calls me? — and begs us to do the same.

C*

Chapter 4

RITES AND CELEBRATIONS

Love all God's creation, the whole of it and every grain of sand. Love every leaf, every ray of God's light. Love the animals, love the plants, love everything. If you love everything, you will perceive the divine mystery of things. And once you have perceived it, you will begin to comprehend it ceaselessly, more and more every day. And you will at last come to love the whole world with an abiding universal love.

— Fyodor Dostoyevsky
The Brothers Karamazov

A LITANY OF THE CIRCLE

Chief Seattle

Leader: Beloved God, known to your creation by a thousand different names, we thank you for giving us power through your Spirit to reveal your life to the world: strengthen, bless, and guide all that we do.

All: Guide us by your grace.

Leader: We thank you for your creation, and pray for the earth that you have given us to cherish and protect; nourish us in your love for all you have made.

All: Guide us by your grace.

Leader: Every part of this earth is sacred,

All: Every shining pine needle, every sandy shore.

Leader: Every mist in the dark woods,

All: Every clearing and every humming insect is holy,

Leader: rocky crest, the juices of the meadow, the beasts, and all the people,

All: All belong to the same family.

Leader: Teach your children that the earth is our mother.

All: Whatever befalls the earth befalls the children of earth.

Leader: The earth's murmur is the voice of our father's father.

All: We are part of the earth and the earth is part of us.

Leader: The rivers are our brothers; they quench our thirst.

All: The perfumed flowers are our sisters.

Leader: The air is precious,

❧ All: For we all share the same breath.

Leader: The wind that gave our grandparents breath also receives
             their last sigh,

❧ All: Gave our children the spirit of life.

Leader: This we know, the earth does not belong to us;

❧ All: We belong to the earth.

Leader: This we know, all things are connected,

❧ All: Like the blood that unites one family.

Leader: All things are connected.

❧ All: Our God is the same God whose compassion is
             equal for all,

Leader: For we did not weave the web of life;

❧ All: We are merely strands of it.

Leader: Whatever we do to the web,

❧ All: We do to ourselves.

Leader: Let us give thanks for the web of life in the circle that
             connects us.

❧ All: Thanks be to God, the God of all, the God known by a
             thousand names. Amen.

This litany is an adaptation made for this collection from Chief Seattle's speech. The great Creator of the world — whether called Wakantanka, Allah, Varuna, God, Great Spirit, or by any other name — is present in every aspect of the created order. For Chief Seattle, every land was a holy land, every being a sacred treasure, woven together in the one cosmic web of life. Thus we give "thanks for the web of life in the circle that connects us."

☾*

WE FACE EAST

A Native American Call to Worship from the Four Directions by an Unknown Author

🦋 FIRST READER:

Come Great Spirit, as we gather in your name. We face East:
To your symbol color — gold for the morning star.
To your animal sign — the eagle which soars ever
upward in the praise of God and calls us to do the same.
To your lessons calling us to balance of mind in the spirit
of humility.
To invoke your spirit of illumination and far-sighted vision.
Help us to love you and one another with our whole
heart, our whole mind, and our whole soul, we pray.

🦋 RESPONSE: Come Holy Spirit, come.

🦋 SECOND READER:

We turn to face South:

To your symbol color — white of clarity and brightness.
To your animal symbol — the quetzal which brings us in
touch with the earth and growing things.
To your lessons calling us to balance of body in the spirit
of a good sense of humor.
To invoke your spirit of innocence, trust and love.
Help us open our eyes to the sacredness of every living
thing, we pray.

❧ Response: Come Holy Spirit, come.

❧ Third Reader:

> We turn to face West:
>> To your symbol color — black, still and quiet.
>> To your symbol — the thunder mighty and purposeful.
>> To your lessons calling us to balance our emotions in the spirit of gentleness and honesty.
>> To invoke your spirit of introspection — seeing within.
>> Give us your strength and the courage to endure, we pray.

❧ Response: Come Holy Spirit, come.

❧ Fourth Reader:

> We turn to face North:
>> To your symbol color — red, the hue of revelation.
>> To your animal symbol — the buffalo, strong and nurturing.
>> To your lessons calling us to the balance of our spirit in harmony with brothers and sisters.
>> To invoke your wisdom and grace of the ages, we pray.

❧ Response: Come Holy Spirit, come.

❧ Fifth Reader:

> We turn to complete the circle and to look:
>> To God who cleanses our earth with snow, wind, and rain;
>> To the Divine Inspiration who fills us with the wideness of God's mercy and lovingly embraces us all; and

To the Holy Spirit who inspires us.

🦋 Response: Come Holy Spirit, come.

This ancient chant, rich in Native American symbolism, has been adapted to a Christian setting. The sacred circle signifies wholeness and harmony. The four directions indicate the four sacred directions of the earth. Together they represent the eternal balance, harmony, and goodness of the world. They are illustrated by various colors, depending upon tribal traditions.

(*

LISTEN TO THE VOICES OF CREATION

Martin Palmer

🦋 Leader: Listen now. Be still and hear. For creation takes up its Maker's call. All creation draws near to God, seeks refuge from the tightening grip of winter, the winter our destruction has wrought; seeks light and warmth to revive that which we have darkened and chilled by our abuse of God's creation. Listen to the voices of creation.

🦋 Air: I the Air come. Breath of life,
wind that moves over the face of the deep.
Bearing rain, I come.
Now the breath of life blows death.
As I pass over the land the broken soil follows me;

a billowing shroud of dust.
When the rain falls, forests and lakes die.
I come, my God.
But what have your people made of me
but a shadow, a dark acidic shadow,
of my God-given glory.
Breathe on your people, breath of God.

All: Breathe on your people, breath of God.

The Waters: We the Waters come, O God, flowing
to meet you, as we have flowed through time,
sustaining the life of all creation.
We come, O God, from our rivers and lakes,
our seas and oceans.
We come, O God, with our dead upon our waves.
Our living struggle against creeping filth
and our mighty creatures flee
before the fury of your people.
Can we ever capture the purity of your will
in the brightness of our waters?
Stir up your people, O God,
to let waters flow with life everlasting.

All: Stir up your people, O God.

The Land: Mountain and valley, hill and plain,
we the Land turn to you, our God,
ground of our ground.
Upon us you set your world,

from us called forth life in many forms.
In our richness you set the forests.
On our fields you sowed the seed of life.
Gone are our forests, worn is the earth.
Silent in their graves lie the riches of your creation.
Gouged out are our mountains,
gone are the curves of our valley.
We who bear your creation seek re-creation.
Plant in your people a love and respect for your land.

❦ All: Plant in your people a love and respect for your land.

Martin Palmer is a writer and a religious adviser to the World Wide Fund for Nature. In his book, Sacred Britain, *he shares his conviction that we need to be engaged in "revisioning our land, drawing from the world's great faiths and indigenous traditions to help us see the true meaning and preciousness of our land . . . to begin to create special places which can reflect not just upon nature but a common purpose for the diversity of people."*

☾*

LITANY OF THE FOUR ELEMENTS

Kate Compston

❦ Leader: Earth, air, fire, and water are traditionally symbols of life. Our "slavery to sin" has meant that these elements may equally carry and contain death.

❦ Life: I am life. I offer earth to share between the daughters and sons of God — soil for bearing plants to sustain the planet's life and yield bread for all people.

A bowl of earth may be presented.

❦ Death: I am death. I take earth away from the many and give it to the few. I exploit and overuse it. I waste its bread, while many starve.

❦ Leader: O God, who wore our clay in Christ, we confess we have not shared the land; we have broken our bond with the earth and one another.

❦ All: Forgive us: we have chosen death. We long for healing: we choose your life.

❦ Life: I offer air to breathe; for the endless energy of the wind, for birds to fly and seeds to blow. Air has no frontiers; we share the breath of life.

Feathers and winged seeds may be presented, or an open-armed gesture made as if to present the air around the speaker.

❧ Death: I fill the air with poisonous fumes which all must breathe,
                 and which claw away the threads of the universe.

❧ Leader: O God, who breathed life into the world,
                 we confess that we have polluted the air;
                 we cannot sense the harmony of your creation.

❧ All: Forgive us: we have chosen death.
                 We long for healing: we choose your life.

❧ Life: I offer fire for life and warmth, for purification and power.
                 Fire draws us together in fellowship, around a meal cooked
                 and shared together.

A candle may be presented.

❧ Death: I use fire for my own violent ends.
                 I burn the forest and choke the air.
                 I give the rich the earth's energy to waste:
                 I deny the poor their fuel to cook with.

❧ Leader: O God, pillar of fire, and Pentecostal flame,
                 we confess our lack of inner fire
                 for your justice to be done,
                 your peace shared on earth.

❧ All: Forgive us: we have chosen death.
                 We long for healing: we choose your life.

❧ Life: I offer water to drink and cleanse;
                 to be the veins and arteries of the land;

I offer strong waves for energy,
and still lakes for calm of spirit.

A bowl of water may be presented,
or the congregation may be sprinkled with water.

Death: I pollute water with waste from the mines and factories,
that it may kill the fish, be bitter to drink, and carry disease.
I withdraw water from the land and make a desert;
I extend the waters of the sea and drown cities.

Leader: O God, fountain of living waters,
we confess that we are cracked cisterns,
lacking stillness to listen to your word,
and energy to act on it.

All: Forgive us: we have chosen death.
We long for healing; we choose your life.

Leader: God of earth, air, fire, and water,
we surrender to you our old humanity:

All: Christ, we would rise with you:
we would be born anew.

Leader: Christ has died: Christ has risen.
We are forgiven: we too may leave the grave.

"Litany of the Four Elements" was written by contemporary writer Kate Compston, who
has worked as an ordained minister of religion, a psychodynamic counselor, a retreat and

workshop leader, and a writer. She has published articles, meditations, prayers, and poems in a variety of books and journals. In this powerful litany she presents the elemental forces of life and death and urges us to choose life.

☾*

A LITANY OF SORROW

Author Unknown

Leader: We have forgotten who we are,
         we have alienated ourselves from the unfolding of the cosmos, we have become estranged from the movements of the earth,
         we have turned our backs on the cycles of life.

❧ Response: We have forgotten who we are and we repent.

Leader: We have sought only our own security,
         we have exploited simply for our own ends,
         we have distorted our knowledge,
         we have abused our power.

❧ Response: We have forgotten who we are and we repent.

Leader: Now the land is barren,
         the waters are poisoned,
         and the air is polluted.

❧ Response: We have forgotten who we are and we repent.

Leader: Now the forests are dying,
               and the creatures are disappearing,
               and human beings are despairing.
Response: We have forgotten who we are and we repent.
Leader: We ask for forgiveness,
               We ask for the gift of remembering,
               We ask for the strength to change.
Response: May we remember who we are.

This litany was first used in a special creation liturgy called An Interfaith Celebration of the Cosmic Story held in Washington, D.C. on September 12, 1993. It cites humankind's alienation from the natural world and asks for three things: forgiveness, the gift of remembering, and the strength to change.

☾*

HOUSE MADE OF DAWN

Navajo Chant

Read with two alternating voices
House made of dawn,
House made of evening light,
House made of rain,
House made of dark mist,
House made of pollen,

House made of grasshoppers,
Dark cloud is at the door.

Thunder roars out of it a dark cloud.
The zigzag lightning stands high upon it.

Great God of the Earth,
I make my offering to you.
I am sorry. *(pause)*
I ask you to —
Restore my feet for me,
Restore my legs for me,
Restore my mind for me,
Restore my voice for me.

Happy may I recover.
Happy may I become cool inside.
Happy may I go forth.

Feeling cool, may I walk.
Healed, may I walk.
With lively feelings, may I walk.
As it was with our elders long ago, may I walk.

Happy may I walk.
Happy with dark clouds, may I walk.

Happy with abundant showers, may I walk.
Happy on the trail of pollen, may I walk.
Being as it was with the elders, may I walk.

May it be beautiful before me.
May it be beautiful behind me.
May it be beautiful above me.
May it be beautiful below me.
May it be beautiful all around me.

In beauty may I lie down at the close of the day.
In beauty may I down at the close of the day.

Until very recently, the Navajo language was oral only and the beautiful poetry was hand-ed down from generation to generation by word of mouth. It is full of symbolism and sentiment that a non-Navajo would not dare to interpret nor claim to fully understand. From this tradi-tion comes "House Made of Dawn," a variation of the "Night Chant," sung for someone on the threshold of death. According to Mark Maryboy, an expert on Navajo culture and tradi-tions, only a medicine man or medicine woman would be permitted to sing it.

☾*

WE JOIN WITH THE EARTH AND EACH OTHER

United Nations Environmental Program

Reader 1:   We join with the earth and each other
To bring new life to the land,
To restore the waters,
To refresh the air.

All: We join with the earth and each other.

Reader 2:   To renew the forests,
To care for the plants,
To protect the creatures.

All: We join with the earth and each other.

Reader 1:   To celebrate the seas,
To rejoice in the sunlight,
To sing the song of the stars.

All: We join with the earth and each other.

Reader 2:   To recall our common destiny on this earth,
To renew our minds,
To reinvigorate our hearts within us.

All: We join with the earth and each other.

Reader 1:   To create the human community,
To promote justice and peace,
For all the children of the earth.

All: We join together as many and diverse expressions
of the one loving mystery:

for the healing of the earth
and the renewal of all life.

This interfaith prayer for the healing of the earth calls us to join together for the renewal of all life.

☾*

NIGHT CHANT

Navajo Chant

Leader: House made of dawn,
                House made of evening light,
                House made of dark cloud where my kindred dwell,
                There may I dwell, there may I wander.

All: There may I dwell, there may I wander.

Leader: The Red Rock House ...

All: There may I wander.

Leader: In the house of happiness,

All: There may I wander.

Leader: Beauty before me,

All: With it I wander.

Leader: Beauty behind me,

All: With it I wander.

Leader: Beauty below me,

❧ All:	With it I wander.
Leader:	Beauty above me,
❧ All:	With it I wander.
Leader:	In old age wandering on the trail of beauty,
❧ All:	Lively may I walk.
Leader:	In old age wandering on the trail of beauty,
❧ All:	Living again, may I walk.
Leader:	is finished.
❧ All:	It is finished in beauty.

The human life cycle is a walk through time. From the dawn of life until "it is finished in beauty," the trail is symbolized in ritual sandpainting, dance, and song. The purpose of Navajo ritual is to carry the person safely and pleasantly along the road in harmony with creation. The "Night Chant," according to Mark Maryboy, is a sacred song sung for a person with a terminal illness who is preparing to finish her or his life in beauty.

☾*

A LITANY OF THANKSGIVING FOR THE AMERICAS

Author Unknown

Leader: For our ancestors who built nations and cultures; who
            thrived and prospered long before the coming of strangers;

for the forfeit of their lives, their homes, their lands, and
their freedoms sacrificed to the rise of new nations and
new worlds.

All: We offer a song of honor and thanks.

Leader: For the wealth of our lands; for the minerals in the earth;
for the plants and waters and animals on the earth; for the
birds, the clouds and rain; for the sun and moon in the sky
and the gifts they gave to our people that enabled the rise
of new world economies.

All: We offer a song of honor and thanks.

Leader: For the many foods coaxed from the heart of Mother
Earth; for the skills we were given to develop foods that
now belong to the world: potatoes, corn, beans, squash,
peanuts, tomatoes, peppers, coffee, cocoa, sugar, and many,
many more.

All: We offer a song of honor and thanks.

Leader: the medicines first discovered by our ancestors now
known to the world: quinine, ipecac, iodine, curare,
petroleum jelly, witch hazel, and others; for the healing skills
of our people and those who now care for us. For tobacco,
sage, sweet grass, and cedar that give spiritual healing by the
power of their meaning.

All: We offer a song of honor and thanks.

Leader: For oceans, streams, rivers, lakes, and other waters of our
lands that provide bountifully for us; for clams, lobsters,
salmon, trout, shrimp, and abalone; for the pathways the
waters have provided.

All: We offer a song of honor and thanks.

Leader: For the friendship that first welcomed all to our shores; for the courage of those who watched their worlds change and disappear and for those who led in the search for new lives; for our leaders today who fight with courage and great heart for us.

All: We offer a song of honor and thanks.

Leader: For the friends who suffered with us and stand with us today to help bring the promise and the hope that the New World meant to their ancestors.

All: We offer a song of honor and thanks.

Leader: For the strength and beauty of our diverse Native cultures; for the traditions that give structure to our lives, that define who we are; for the skills of our artists and crafts people and the gifts of their hands.

All: We offer a song of honor and thanks.

Leader: For the spirituality and vision that gave our people the courage and faith to endure; that brought many to an understanding and acceptance of the love of Christ, our brother and savior.

All: We offer a song of honor and thanks.

Leader: Accept, O God, Creator, our honor song, and make our hearts thankful for what we have been given. Make us humble for what we have taken. Make us glad as we return some measure of what we have been given. Strengthen our faith and make us strong in the service of our people, in the name of our Brother and Savior, Jesus Christ, your Son, in the power of the Holy Spirit. Amen.

This litany, written for a service in the National Cathedral in Washington commemorating the 500th anniversary of Columbus's voyage to the Americas, reminds us of the many and huge contributions Native Americans have made to the world community.

C*

WE LIVE IN RELATION TO ALL THINGS

Author Unknown

Leader: We live in relation to all things,
                    all things live within us.
Response: We rejoice in all life.
Leader: We live by the sun,
                    we move with the stars.
Response: We rejoice in all life.
Leader: We eat from the earth,
                    we drink from the rain,
                    we breathe from the air.
Response: We rejoice in all life.
Leader: We share with all the creatures,
                    we have strength through their gifts.
Response: We rejoice in all life.
Leader: We depend on the forests and the rivers,
                    we have knowledge through their secrets.
Response: We rejoice in all life.

🦋 Response: We have the privilege of seeing and understanding,
we have the responsibility of caring and protecting,
we have the joy of celebrating.

Leader: We rejoice in all life.

🦋 Response: We are full of the grace of creation.
We are grateful, we are grateful.
We rejoice in all life.

This responsive litany of promise was used as part of a creation liturgy called an "Interfaith Celebration of the Cosmic Story." It echoes these words attributed to Chief Seattle: "All things are connected like the blood that connects us all. We did not weave the web of life, we are merely strands in it. . . . We are all brothers and sisters, together woven into this sacred earth."

☾*

LET THE LIGHT FALL WARM AND RED ON THE ROCK

A Liturgy at Sunset

Alison Newall, Iona Community

Opening Litany

Leader: Let the light fall warm and red on the rock,
Let the birds sing their evening song

	And let God's people say Amen.
All:	Amen.
Leader:	Let the tools be stored away,
	Let the work be over and done
	And let God's people say Amen.
All:	Amen.
Leader:	Let the flowers close and the stars appear,
	Let hearts be glad and minds be calm
	And let God's people say Amen.
All:	Amen.

Psalm or Reading (concerning creation)

Confession

Leader:	O God, your fertile earth is slowly being stripped of its riches.
All:	Open our eyes to see.
Leader:	O God, your living waters are slowly being choked with chemicals.
All:	Open our eyes to see.
Leader:	O God, your clean air is slowly being filled with pollutants.
All:	Open our eyes to see.
Leader:	O God, your creatures are slowly dying and your people are suffering.
All:	Open our eyes to see.

Leader: God our Maker, so move us by the
            wonder of your creation,

🦋 All: That we repent and care more deeply.

Leader: So move us to grieve the loss of life,

🦋 All: That we learn to cherish and protect your world.

Chant or Song

(During which there will be an action in which we
commit ourselves to caring for God's earth or celebrate the
goodness of God's earth.)

Prayer of Thanksgiving

Song

Closing Responses

Leader: This we know, the earth does not belong to us.

🦋 All: We belong to the earth.

Leader: This we know, all things are connected,

🦋 All: Like the blood that unites one family.

Leader: This we know, we did not weave the web of life,

🦋 All: We are merely a strand of it.

Leader: This we know, whatever we do to the web,

🦋 All: We do to ourselves.

Leader: Let us give thanks for the gift of creation.

All: Let us give thanks that all things hold together
     in the creator God of the universe.

Blessing

Leader: Bless us, O God,
     The moon that is above us,
     The earth that is beneath us,
     Your image deep within us.
All: Amen.

The natural setting for the Iona Community's liturgy reproduced here is a place of great natural beauty out of doors as evening approaches. The liturgy invites us to acknowledge that humankind — our kind — has stripped the land of its resources, choked the waters with chemicals, and polluted the atmosphere. It offers participants the opportunity to dedicate themselves afresh to caring for the earth and celebrating the goodness of creation.

☾*

FOR COCONUTS AND TARO

A Litany from the Pacific

Leader: For the earth, and all that is a part of it,

🦋 Response: We praise you, Holy God.

Leader: For rocks, signs of your strength and your steadfast love,

🦋 Response: We praise you, Holy God.

Leader: For shells, signs of your variety and your joy
in creating this world, which you have given to our care,

🦋 Response: We praise you, Holy God.

Leader: For coconuts and taro, signs of your providence to us,

🦋 Response: We praise you, Holy God.

Leader: For the birds, signs of the freedom that is ours when we
recognize that we are your children,

🦋 Response: We praise you, Holy God.

Leader: For the fish of the sea and the animals that walk on the
land, a reminder to us that the new earth is to be a place
where your people live, work, and share in peace,

🦋 Response: We praise you, Holy God.

Leader: For the variety of insects, their spontaneity and ways of
growth, signs of dying and rising to new life that is your
central message,

🦋 Response: We praise you, Holy God.

Leader: For the similarities of one group of people to another,

signs of our unity in the one fold following the one
shepherd of all,

❦ Response: We praise you, Holy God.

    Leader: For the difference between one group of people and
another expressed in the islands through the variety of
language, tradition, custom, denomination, signs of the
challenge of your word,

❦ Response: We praise you, Holy God.

    Leader: For the people present at this celebration, who by their
commitment, readiness to learn and listen, and openness of
heart and mind are signs of your hope for the future of your
creation,

❦ Response: We praise you, Holy God.

*The Pacific Islands, the vast region also known as Oceania, include two thousand islands
in more than thirty major groupings. Extremely diverse culturally and linguistically, the six
million people who call Oceania home share one common sea and thus one common destiny.
The sea is both nourishing and threatening; it is a blessing and a curse. Whereas most of us
look outwards to solid earth, these people look to the sea. This reality affects everything.*

☾*

THE TREES SHALL CLAP THEIR HANDS

A Litany before the Clear-Cutting of a Forest

Leader: As we face the destruction of this forest, let us thank God, with the Psalmist and Prophets, for this wonderful creation; let us hear God's warning of judgment on those who destroy it and rejoice in the hope of its future.

Celebration of Creation

Leader: The earth is the Lord's and everything in it; the world and all who live therein.

All: God has founded it upon the seas and established it upon the waters. (Psalm 24:1–2)

Leader: The trees of the Lord are watered abundantly, the cedars of Lebanon which he planted.

All: In them the birds build their nests; the stork has her home in the fir trees. (Psalm 104:16–17)

Leader: Who shall ascend the hill of the Lord and stand in God's holy place?

All: Those with clean hands and pure hearts who do not swear deceitfully. (Psalm 24:3–4)

Judgment on Those Who Destroy the Environment

Leader: Let us hear the warning words of Isaiah:

Woe to those who call evil good and good evil, who call
darkness light and light darkness.

❧ All: Who call bitter sweet and sweet bitter.

  Leader: Woe to those who are wise in their own eyes.

❧ All: And shrewd in their own sight. (Isaiah *5:20–21*)

  Leader: On a bare hill raise a signal; cry aloud to them.

❧ All: Wave the hand to them to enter the gates. (Isaiah *13:2*)

❧ First Reader:

The Lord enters into judgment
with the elders and princes of the people;
"It is you who have devoured the vineyard.
The spoils of the poor are in your houses.
What do you mean by crushing my people,
by grinding the face of the poor?"
Says the Lord God of Hosts. (Isaiah *3:14–15*)

❧ Second Reader:

Woe to those who join house to house,
who add field to field,
until there is no room,
and you are made to dwell alone
in the midst of the land.
The Lord of hosts has sworn in my hearing;
"Surely many houses shall become desolate,
large and beautiful houses, without inhabitants."
(Isaiah *5:8–9*)

❧ Third Reader:

> Woe to those who make unjust laws that oppress my
> people, and the writers who keep writing oppression,
> That is how you keep the poor from having their rights and
> from getting justice (Isaiah *10:1–2*)

❧ Fourth Reader:

> Whom have you noticed and reviled? Against
> whom have you raised your voice and haughtily
> lifted your eyes?

❧ All: Against the Holy One of Israel.

❧ Fourth Reader:

> Who do you think you have been insulting and ridiculing?
> You have been disrespectful of me, the holy God of Israel.
> You sent your servants to boast to me that with all your
> chariots you conquered the highest mountains of Lebanon.
> You boasted that you cut down the tallest cedars and the
> finest cypress trees, and that you reached the deepest parts
> of the forest. (Isaiah *37:23–24*)

   Leader: Thus says the Lord,

❧ Fourth Reader:

> "Because you have raged against me
> and I have received the report of your arrogance
> I will put a hook through your nose and a bit in your mouth
> and I will turn you back by the same way you came."
> (Isaiah *37:29*)

Hope for Creation

Leader: But the God of justice gives us hope for the future.

❧ Fifth Reader:

> For there is hope for a tree,
> if it be cut down, that it will sprout again,
> and that its shoots will not cease.

Leader: Though its roots grow old in the earth,
> and its stump dies in the ground.

❧ All: Yet at the scent of water it will bud and will put forth
> branches like a young plant.

Leader: The earth is set firmly in its place and cannot be moved.
> The trees in the forest will shout for joy. (Psalm *96:10,12*)

❧ All: God will judge the world with truth and justice.

Leader: The Lord has ended the power of evil rulers who angrily
> oppressed the peoples and never stopped persecuting the
> nations they had conquered. The cypress trees and the
> cedars of Lebanon rejoice and say, (Isaiah. *13:5,8*)

❧ All: "Now that you have been laid low, no woodsman comes to
> cut us down." (Isaiah *14:8*)

Leader: You shall go out in joy,
> and be led forth in peace;
> the mountains and hills before you
> shall burst into singing.

❧ All: And all the trees of the field shall clap their hands.
> (Isaiah *55:12*)

Leader: We thank you, Lord, for this forest.

🍃 All: We thank you Lord.

Leader: We are sad that the hill has been shaved and the trees have been cut down and not replanted.

🍃 All: We are sad.

🍃 Leader: But we know that the trees of the forest shall one day clap their hands. Alleluia.

🍃 All: The trees of the forest shall clap their hands. Alleluia!

(Everyone claps.)

This litany was written to mark the destruction of Kamuruana Hill in Kenya, which had been completely cleared of all its trees. On May 19, 1991, the entire congregation of Trinity Church, Mutuma, Kirinyaqa, walked in procession to the foot of the hill to participate in the liturgy. This process of creating a liturgy to fit a specific situation serves two purposes: it draws public attention to the issue at hand and it involves the people directly in seeking a solution.

ℭ*

RESTORE OUR EARTH HOUSEHOLD

The Free Church of Berkeley

After each petition read by the leader, the response is: "Restore our earth household."

🍃 Restore our earth household —

🍃 All powers of being, restore our earth household —

Air and wind, blowing out the smog of our self-poisoning —

Snow and rain, washing down the poisons of our combustion —

Salts of the sea, decomposing life-killing chemicals —

Fire and light, breaking down the products of industry —

Crabgrass and dandelion, cracking waterproofed surfaces —

Worms and wood lice, reconverting all foreign materials —

Rust and decay — restoring all metals to earth loam —

Plankton of the deep, feeding the great whales —

Rivers and streams, purifying the land's body —

Termites and rot, leveling all settlements —

Squirrels and all rodents, distributing acorns —

Deer and buffalo, in cooperation with grasslands —

Bear and hawk and all carnivores, completing the cycle —

Spirit of John Muir, keeper of the garden, marching beside us —

Spirit of Johnny Appleseed, planter of Eden, marching beside us —

Yin and Yang, male and female principles of creation —

Buddha, the compassionate, surviving the cycle of dying —

Adam and Eve, first parents in the paradise of Eden —

Angels and guardians of spirits, watching over this planet —

Seeds of life in the sun, in the space between the stars —

Our galactic mother, enfolding the planet in her spiral arms —

Billion-year heartbeat of the cosmic expansion —

Nameless energy upholding the universe —

Eternal principle of non-violence —

Jesus our loving brother, non-violence in our own flesh —

All who build a new world in the vacant lots of the old —

This responsive reading was taken from a longer liturgy entitled "Earth Rebirth."
It was written for the dedication of the People's Park in Berkeley, California, on May 11, 1969.
In adapting it for this collection, John Pairman Brown, the principal author, says, "I do appre-
ciate your resonating to those old rhythms of ours. I still keep thinking about cosmology."

☾*

GOD OF ALL POWER

A Litany of Petitions and Thanksgiving for God's Creation

Anne Rowthorn

Each participant formulates one petition, based on their concerns for the environment,
concluding with the following words: "Holy One, have mercy upon us."

Leader: God of all power, Ruler of the Universe, you are worthy
              of praise. At your command all things came to be: the
              vast expanse of interstellar space, galaxies, suns, the planets
              in their courses, and this fragile earth, our island home. By
              your will they were created and have their being. From the
              primal elements you brought forth the human race, and
              blessed us with memory, reason, and skill. But we turned
              against you, and betrayed your trust; we turned against one
              another. Again and again, you call us to return. Today you
              call us to return as we turn to you in prayer:

Read your petition. At the end say:

Holy One, have mercy upon us…

All: And incline our hearts to follow in your way.
Leader: Almighty God, maker of all things, you open your hand
            and satisfy the desire of every living creature on earth. We
            praise you for crowning your fields and forests, seas and
            skies with blessings. Open our eyes to behold their beauty
            and our hearts to love and care for your holy creation.
            Amen.

*This litany format was developed for use in Caring for Creation, the ecology and justice
course I teach at the Hartford Seminary in Connecticut. It is appropriate for use after a day-
long workshop or class on environmental responsibility.*

☾*

A BUDDHIST LITANY FOR PEACE

Thich Nhat Nanh

As we are together praying for Peace,
    let us be truly with each other.…
(silence)
    Let us be aware of the source of being common to us all
        and to all living things.

(silence)

Evoking the presence of the Great Compassion,

let us fill our hearts with our own compassion —

towards ourselves and towards all living beings.

(silence)

Let us pray that all living beings realize

that they are all brothers and sisters,

all nourished from the same source of life.

(silence)

Let us pray that we ourselves

cease to be the cause of suffering to each other.

(silence)

Let us plead with ourselves

to live in a way which will not deprive other living beings

of air, water, food, shelter, or the chance to live.

(silence)

With humility, with awareness of the existence of life,

and of the sufferings that are going on around us,

let us pray for the establishment of

peace in our hearts and on earth. Amen.

Thich Nhat Hanh is, above all and in every sense, a peacemaker. The Dalai Lama, in introducing Hanh's book, Peace Is Every Step, *said, "Although attempting to bring about world peace through internal transformation of individuals is difficult, it is the only way. Peace must first be developed within an individual. And I believe that love, compassion, and altruism are the fundamental basis for peace. Once these qualities are developed within an individual, he*

*or she is able to create an atmosphere of peace and harmony. This atmosphere can be expand-
ed and extended from the individual to the community and eventually to the whole world."*

C*

O GOD OF THE GREAT WATERS, PROTECT US

Rig-Veda

Leader: Ceaseless are the waters, ceaselessly flowing, ceaselessly
    cleansing, never sleeping,
    Ceaselessly flowing in channels of the earth,
    Rising from the middle of the flood flowing to
    the parent the sea.

All: O God of the great waters, protect us.

Leader: There are waters which come from heaven, waters dug
    from the earth, and waters gushing free,
    By themselves, shining waters, ceaselessly purifying,
    ceaselessly flowing to the ocean.

All: O God of the great waters, protect us.

Leader: O God, presiding over the great waters, you know truth
    from falsehood,
    You are ceaselessly purifying.

All: O God of the great waters, protect us.

Leader:	All people drink and draw life and strength from the waters that ceaselessly flow through all creation and all time throughout all ages.
❧ All:	O God of the great waters, protect us.

From the Rig-Veda, the oldest of Hinduism's sacred scriptures, this was probably written by Aryan tribesmen. The Rig-Veda is full of poems of wonder and praise celebrating the gifts of nature and human beings' relationships with the natural world. The Vedic sage believed that humankind could only live happily on this earth by living the Vedic values of truth, justice, and spiritual discipline.

☾*

IN THE BEGINNING, GOD MADE THE WORLD
A Morning Liturgy

Alison Newall, Iona Community

Opening Litany (all standing)

Leader:	In the beginning, God made the world:
❧ Women:	Made it and mothered it,
❧ Men:	Shaped it and fathered it.
❧ Women:	Filled it with seeds and signs of fertility,

❧ Men: Filled it with love and its folk with ability.
Leader: All that is green, blue, deep, and growing,
❧ All: God's is the hand that created you.
Leader: All that is tender, firm, fragrant, and curious,
❧ All: God's is the hand that created you.
Leader: All that crawls, flies, swims, walks, or is motionless,
❧ All: God's is the hand that created you.
Leader: All that speaks, sings, cries, laughs, or keeps silent,
❧ All: God's is the hand that created you.
Leader: All that suffers, lacks, limps, or longs for an end,
❧ All: God's is the hand that created you.
Leader: The world belongs to the Lord.
❧ All: the earth and all its people are his.

A Song or Hymn

Prayer of Approach (all sit or kneel)

Leader: Let us pray.
             Before the world began,
             when everything was shapeless,
             You were there...
             hovering over the chaos,
             planning the texture, the taste,
             the sight and the sound of things,
             balancing the opposites,

weaving the rainbow,

turning the random into the real,

All: And for this we praise you.

Leader: Before we began,

when, in the womb, we were shapeless,

You were there...

calling us your own;

planning the nature and novelty in us,

weaning our potentials,

making us unique,

turning the random into the real,

All: And for this we praise you.

Leader: And even now,

now when we dream dreams,

or puzzle over the future.

Now, when our ideals are challenged

and the second best becomes attractive,

You are there...

upsetting our easiness,

contradicting our compromises,

replacing our narrow vision

with the sight and sound and taste of a better life,

picking up the loose stitches of our devotion,

turning the random into the real,

All: And for this we praise you.

Leader: And it will always be so.

For you did not say you were the answer.

You said you were the way;

you did not ask us to succeed.

You asked us to be faithful;

you did not promise us paradise tomorrow.

You said you would be with us to the end of the world,

turning the random into the real.

❧ All: And for all this we praise you, now and forever. Amen.

The Word of God

(This may be preceded and/or followed by a song, chorus, or chant.)

❧ Reader: The scripture read is found in...(book, chapter, verse)

Let us listen to the Word of God.

(The reading)

This is the Word (or Gospel) of our God.

❧ All: Thanks be to God.

Prayers for the Coming of the Kingdom

Leader: Let us pray for the breaking in of God's kingdom

in our world,

❧ All: Your kingdom come, your will be done.

Leader: Where nations budget for war

while Christ says, "Put away your sword,"

❧ All: Your kingdom come, your will be done.

Leader: Where countries waste food and covet fashion

while Christ says, "I was hungry...I was thirsty..."

❧ All:	Your kingdom come, your will be done.
Leader:	Where powerful governments claim their policies are heaven-blessed,
	while Scripture proclaims that God has no favorites,
❧ All:	Your kingdom come, your will be done.
Leader:	Where Christians seek the kingdom in the shape of their own church,
	as if Christ had come to build and not break down barriers,
❧ All:	Your kingdom come, your will be done.
Leader:	Where women who speak up for their dignity are treated with scorn or contempt,
❧ All:	Your kingdom come, your will be done.
Leader:	Where men try hard to be tough, because they're afraid to be tender,
❧ All:	Your kingdom come, your will be done.
Leader:	Where we, obsessed with being adult, forget to become like children,
❧ All:	Your kingdom come, your will be done.
Leader:	Where our prayers falter, our faith weakens, our light grows dim,
❧ All:	Your kingdom come, your will be done.
Leader:	Where Jesus Christ calls us,
❧ All:	Your kingdom come, your will be done.
Leader:	Holy God, You have declared that your kingdom is among us,

Open our eyes to see it,
our ears to hear it,
our hearts to hold it,
our hands to serve it.
This we pray in Jesus' name. Amen.

A Song or Hymn (all standing)

Closing Responses

Leader: For all that God can do within us;
              for all that God can do without us,

All: Thanks be to God.

Leader: For all in whom Christ lived before us;
              for all in whom Christ lives beside us,

All: Thanks be to God.

Leader: For all the Spirit wants to bring us,
              for where the Spirit wants to send us,

All: Thanks be to God.

Leader: Listen.
              Christ has promised to be with us
              in the world as in our worship.

All: Amen, we go to meet him.

Blessing

Leader: May God bless us;
              May God keep us in the Spirit's care
              And lead our lives with love.

❧ All: May God's warm welcome shine from our hearts
and Christ's own peace prevail through this and every day,
till greater life shall call. Amen.

This liturgy is a gift from the Iona Community in Scotland. Saint Columba (ca. 521–597), a monk from a noble Irish family, impelled by missionary zeal, left his home with twelve companions and in 563 established himself on Iona, a remote island off the western coast of Scotland where only a thin mist separates the sea from the sky. Columba founded a religious community that became an important center for Celtic Christianity

☾*

A DIVINE VOICE SINGS
THROUGH ALL CREATION

General Conference of American Rabbis

Leader: How wonderful, O God, are the works of your hands!
The heavens declare your glory, the arch of the sky
displays your handiwork.

❧ Response: The heavens declare the glory of God.

Leader: In your love you have given us the power to behold the
beauty of your world, robed in all its splendor. The sun and
the stars, they valleys and hills, the rivers and lakes — all
disclose your presence.

🦋 Response: The earth reveals God's eternal presence.

  Leader: The roaring breakers of the sea tell of your might; the beasts of the field and the birds of the air bespeak your wondrous will.

🦋 Response: Life comes forth by God's creative will.

  Leader: In your goodness you have made us able to hear the music of the world. The raging of the winds, the whispering of trees in the wood, and the precious voices of loved ones reveal to us that you are in our midst.

🦋 Response: A divine voice sings through all creation.

The Creator God, the grand architect and builder of the universe, is revealed through the majesty of creation, even "the raging of the winds." We need only to clear our minds, calm our bodies, and open our ears so that we may hear the sweet music of the spheres as the "divine voice sings through all creation."

☾*

CREATION'S SONG OF PRAISE

Song of the Three Young Men

Invocation (All)

Glorify God, all you works of creation.
Praise and highly exalt the Holy One for ever.
In the firmament of God's power, glorify the Holy One,
praise and highly exalt God for ever.

The Cosmic Order

Side 1:   Glorify God, you angels and all powers of creation,
         O heavens and all waters above the heavens.

Side 2:   Sun and moon and stars of the sky, glorify the Holy One,
         praise and highly exalt God for ever.

Side 1:   Glorify God, every shower of rain and fall of dew,
         all winds and fire and heat.

Side 2:   Winter and summer, glorify the Creator,
         praise and highly exalt God for ever.

Side 1:   Glorify God, O chill and cold,
         drops of dew and flakes of snow.

Side 2:   Frost and cold, ice and sleet, glorify the Creator,
         praise and highly exalt God for ever.

Side 1:   Glorify God, O nights and days,
         O shining light and enfolding dark.

Side 2:   Storm clouds and thunderbolts, glorify the Creator,
         praise and highly exalt God for ever.

The Earth and Its Creatures

Side 1:   Let the earth glorify God,
         praise and highly exalt the Creator God forever.

Side 2:   Glorify the God, O mountains and hills,
         and all that grows upon the earth,
         praise and highly exalt the Holy One for ever.

Side 1:   Glorify God, O springs of water, seas, and streams,
         O whales and all that moves in the waters.

Side 2:   All birds of the air, glorify the Creator,
                praise and highly exalt God for ever.
Side 1:   Glorify God, O beasts of the wild,
                and all you flocks and herds.
Side 2:   O men and women everywhere, glorify the Creator,
                praise and highly exalt God for ever.

The People of God

Side 1:   Let the people of God glorify their Creator,
                praise and highly exalt God for ever.
Side 2:   Glorify God, O priests and servants of the Holy One,
                praise and highly exalt God for ever.
Side 1:   Glorify God, O spirits and souls of the righteous,
                praise and highly exalt the Holy One for ever.
Side 2:   You that are holy and humble of heart, glorify the Creator,
                praise and highly exalt God forever.

Doxology (All)

Let us glorify God: Creator, Redeemer,
    and Sustainer of the universe,
praise and highly exalt God for ever.
In the firmament of God's power, glorify the Creator,
praise and highly exalt the Holy One for ever.

*Included in the Apocryphal literature of the Bible is the "Story of the Three Young Men,"
entitled here "Creation's Song of Praise." It is the final song of three Jewish captives in*

Babylon, who were about to be punished for their refusal to worship the idolatrous golden image. At the moment of their death in the fiery furnace they sang out their song that is an exhortation to all living creatures and every aspect of creation to praise God, the creator of all. This is the most comprehensive blessing to be found anywhere in Biblical literature.

C*

PRAISE OF GOD'S CREATION IN CHANTS AND ECHOES

An Orthodox Creation Liturgy

Metropolitan Tryphon, Orthodox Archbishop of Turkestanov

Chant 1:

Incorruptible God, your right hand controls the whole course of human life, according to the decrees of your providence. We give you thanks for all your blessings, known and unknown; for our earthly life and for the heavenly joys of your kingdom which is to come. Henceforth extend your mercies toward us as we sing: Glory to you O Holy God, from age to age!

Echo 1:

I was born a weak, defenseless child, but your angel, spreading her radiant wings, guarded my cradle. From my birth, your love has illumined my paths, and has wondrously guided me towards the light of eternity. From my first days until now, the generous gifts of your providence have been wondrously showered upon me. I give you thanks, and with all those who have come to know you, I exclaim:

Glory to you for calling me into being,
Glory to you for spreading out before me
        the beauty of the universe,
Glory to you for revealing to me heaven and earth,
Glory to your eternity within this fleeting world,
Glory to you for mercies seen and unseen,
Glory to you for every sigh of my sorrow,
Glory to you for every step in my life's
        journey, for every moment of joy,
Glory to you, O Holy God, from age to age.

Chant 2:

O Holy God, how lovely it is to be your guest:
Breeze full of scent; mountains reaching to the skies;
Waters like a boundless mirror,
Reflecting the sun's golden rays and the scudding clouds.
All nature murmurs mysteriously, breathing depths of
tenderness, Birds and beasts bear the imprint of your love,
Blessed are you, Mother Earth, in your overwhelming loveliness,
Which wakens our yearning for happiness that will last
        for ever.
All creation sings to you: Alleluia!

Echo 2:

You brought us into this life as into an enchanted paradise. We have seen the sky, like a deep blue cup ringing with birds in the azure heights. We have listened to the soothing murmur of the forest and the sweet-sounding music of the waters. We have tasted fragrant fruit of fine flavor and sweet-scented honey. How pleasant is our stay with you on earth: it is a joy to be your guest.

Glory to you for the feast day of life,
Glory to you for the perfume of lilies and roses,
Glory to you for each different taste of berry and fruit,
Glory to you for the sparkling silver of early morning dew,
Glory to you for each smiling, peaceful awakening,
Glory to you, O Holy God, from age to age.

Chant 3:

In your strength each flower gives out its scent-sweet perfume, delicate color, beauty of the whole universe revealed in the tiniest thing. Glory and honor to God the Giver of life, who covers the fields with their carpet of flowers, crowns the plains with harvest of gold and the blue of cornflowers, and our souls with the joy of contemplating the Holy God of earth and sky. O be joyful and sing to God: Alleluia!

Echo 3:

How glorious you are in the triumph of spring, when every

creature awakes to new life and joyfully sings your praises with a thousand tongues: you are the source of life, the conqueror of death. By the light of the moon nightingales sing; the plains and the woods put on their wedding garments, white as snow.

Glory to you for bringing from the darkness of the earth an
          endless variety of colors, tastes and scents,
Glory to you for the warmth and tenderness of
          the world of nature,
Glory to you for surrounding us with tens of thousands of
          your works,
Glory to you for the depth of your wisdom:
          the whole world is a living sign of it,
Glory to you; on our knees we kiss the traces
          of your unseen hand,
Glory to you for setting before us the dazzling light
          of your eternal beauty,
Glory to you for the hope of the imperishable
          splendor of immortality,
Glory to you, O Holy God, from age to age.

Chant 4:

How filled with sweetness are those whose thoughts dwell on you. How life-giving your Holy Word. To speak with you is more soothing than anointing with oil, sweeter than the honeycomb. Praying to you refreshes us and gives us wings. Our hearts overflow with warmth; a majesty filled with wisdom permeates nature and all of life. Where you are not, there is only emptiness. Where you are, the soul is filled with abundance, and a song resounds like a mighty torrent: Alleluia!

Echo 4:

When over the earth the light of the setting sun fades away, when the peace of eternal sleep and the quiet of the declining day reign over all, we see your dwelling place like tents filled with light, reflecting the shapes of the clouds at dusk. Fiery and purple, gold and blue, they speak prophet-like of the ineffable beauty of your heavenly court, and solemnly call: let us go to the Holy One!

Glory to you in the quiet of evening,
Glory to you, covering the world with deep peace,
Glory to you for the last ray of the setting sun,
Glory to you for the rest of blissful sleep,
Glory to you for your mercy in the midst of darkness,
     when the whole world has parted company with us,
Glory to you for the tender emotion of a soul moved to prayer,
Glory to you for the pledge of our awakening on the day
     which has no evening,
Glory to you, O Holy God, from age to age.

Chant 5:

The storms of life do not frighten those whose hearts are ablaze with the light of your flame. Outside is the darkness of the whirlwind, the terror of the howling storm. But in their souls reign quiet and light. The Holy One is there, and the heart sings: Alleluia!

Echo 5:

We see your heaven glowing with stars. How rich you are, how much light is yours! Eternity watches us by the rays of the distant stars. The Holy One is always with us, God's loving hand protects us wherever we go.

Glory to you for the care you take for us at all times,
Glory to you for the people your Providence gave us to meet,
Glory to you for the love of dear ones, the faithfulness of
          friends,
Glory to you for the gentleness of the animals of the earth,
Glory to you for light-filled moments of life,
Glory to you for the radiant joy of living, moving and seeing,
Glory to you, O Holy God, from age to age.

Chant 6:

How great and close you are in the powerful track of the storm; how mighty your right arm in the blinding flash of the lightening; how awesome is your greatness! The voice of the Holy One is over the fields and amid the rustling forests, the voice of God is in the birth of thunder and of rain, the voice of God is over the many waters. Praise to you in the roar of mountains ablaze. You shake the earth like a garment. You pile up to the sky the waves of the sea. Praise to you, bringing low the pride of humankind, bringing from the hearts of men and women everywhere cries of repentance: Alleluia!

Echo 6:

> When the lightening flash has lit up the feasting-hall, how fee-
> ble seems the light of lamps. Amid the strongest joys of exis-
> tence, you suddenly flash in our souls. Passionately our souls
> run after you.
>
> Glory to you, the goal in whom humankind's highest dreams
> come true,
> Glory to you, for our unquenchable thirst for communion
> with God,
> Glory to you, making us dissatisfied with material things,
> Glory to you, clothing us with the finest rays of light,
> Glory to you, destroying the power of the spirits of darkness,
> dooming all evil to destruction,
> Glory to you for the joy of hearing your voice, for the happi-
> ness of your presence and of living in your love,
> Glory to you, O Holy God, from age to age.

Chant 7:

> In the wondrous blending of sounds it is your call we hear. In
> the harmony of many voices, stirred by musical tones, dazzled
> by art's creativeness, we learn from you the splendor of
> melody and song and receive a foretaste of the coming king-
> dom. All true beauty draws the soul towards you in powerful
> invocation, and makes us sing triumphantly: Alleluia!

Echo 7:

> The outpouring of the Holy Spirit enlightens the thoughts of

artists, poets, and scientists. Their great minds receive from you prophetic insights into your laws, and reveal to us the depth of your creative wisdom. How great you are in all that you have created, how great you are in the people of earth!

Glory to you, showing your unfathomable might in the laws
        of the universe!
Glory to you, for all nature is permeated by your laws,
Glory to you for what you have revealed to us in your goodness,
Glory to you for all that remains hidden from
        us in your wisdom,
Glory to you for the inventiveness of the human mind,
Glory to you for the invigorating effort of work,
Glory to you for the tongues of fire which bring inspiration,
Glory to you, O Holy God, from age to age.

Chant 8:

Why is it that on a feast day the whole of nature mysteriously smiles? Why does an incomparable lightness then fill our hearts? The very air at the altar and in God's house becomes luminous. It is the breath of grace, the reflection of the glory of Mount Tabor; heaven and earth are singing this praise: Alleluia!

Echo 8:

When you inspire us to serve our neighbors, and make humility shine in our souls, deep-piercing rays of light fall into the

hearts of each one of us. Your rays glow, like iron in a furnace.
We see your face, mysterious and elusive.

Glory to you, transfiguring our lives with deeds of love,

Glory to you, making wonderfully sweet each one of your
        commandments,

Glory to you, present in fragrant compassion,

Glory to you, sending us failures and afflictions to make us
        sensitive to other people's sufferings,

Glory to you, promising high rewards for
        precious wholesome deeds,

Glory to you, welcoming the impulse of our heart's love,

Glory to you, for raising love above everything on earth,

Glory to you, O Holy God, from age to age.

Chant 9:

No one can put together what has crumbled into dust, but you, O Holy God, can heal those whose ideals have become twisted; you give the soul its former beauty long since lost. With you, nothing is hopeless. You are love. You are the creator and redeemer of all things. We praise you with this unending song: Alleluia!

Echo 9:

O God, you know the fall of proud Lucifer. Save me through the power of your grace; do not allow me to fall away from you, do not allow me to doubt you. Sharpen my ear, that at every minute of my life I may hear your mysterious voice. You who are everywhere present, hear me when I call to you.

Glory to you for providential circumstances,
Glory to you for helpful forebodings,
Glory to you for the teaching of your secret voice,
Glory to you for revelations you give us waking and dreaming,
Glory to you for scattering our vain imaginations,
Glory to you, freeing us from the fire of passions
        through suffering,
Glory to you, who for our salvation, brings down
        our proudness of heart,
Glory to you, O Holy God, from age to age.

Chant 10:

Beyond the icy sequence of the ages, we feel the warmth of
your divine breath. Throughout all eons of time and space
your creatures continuously sing your praise: Alleluia!

Echo 10:

Blessed are those who will share your mystical supper in your
realm; but even here on earth you have granted us blessedness.
How many times with your divine hand, you have offered us
your body and blood. How many times we have received these
sacred gifts and felt your ineffable and supernatural love.

Glory to you for the inconceivable and life-giving
        power of grace,
Glory to you who established havens of peace
        in a tormented world,

Glory to you for giving us new birth in the
　　　　life-giving waters of baptism,
Glory to you, restoring to those who repent
　　　　purity white as the unstained lily,
Glory to you, unfathomable reservoir of forgiveness,
Glory to you for the cup of life, for the bread of eternal joy,
Glory to you who raise us to heaven,
Glory to you, O Holy God, from age to age.

Chant 11:

More than once have we seen the reflection of your glory in the faces of those hovering on the threshold of death. What beauty, what heavenly joy shines through them. How light their features, how present you are in them. This is the triumph of happiness and peace finding their rest in you. In their silence they are calling to you. At the hour of our deaths, illumine our souls: Alleluia!

Echo 11:

How poor is our praise before you! We have not yet heard the song of the cherubim, a joy reserved to the souls on high, but we know the praises nature sings to you. In the moonlit silence of winter the whole earth offers you prayer, wrapped in its white mantle of snow, sparkling like diamonds. We see the rising sun rejoice in you and hear the chorus of birds raise a hymn of glory. We hear the forest rustling in your honor, the winds singing to you. The waters murmur and the processions

of the stars proclaim you as they move in harmony forever
across the infinity of space.
Glory to you, who has shown us the light,
Glory to you loving us with a deep, unfathomable love,
Glory to you blessing us with light, with a
              host of angels and saints,
Glory to you, most Holy God, revealing to us your realm,
Glory to you, Holy Spirit, life-giving sun
              of the world to come,
Glory to you for all things,
Glory to you, O Holy God, from age to age.

Chant 12:

Glory to you, God of earth and all the stars, God of the Exodus, God
of the jubilee, making immortal all that is life-giving and good. May every
creature of earth and heaven enter into your eternal joy, praising you and
singing unceasingly the triumphal hymn: Alleluia! Alleluia! Alleluia!

*The Orthodox expression of Christianity offers a unique vision of the material creation
and humankind's place in it, one which can restore a true relationship with God and the world.
"Praise of God's Creation in Chants and Echoes" is a long reading. Relax into it, slowly
absorbing its comprehensive depth of praise. Use the chants and echoes to alternate men and
women's voices, or alternate adult voices with the voices of children and youth.*

☪*

PRAISE TO THE BREATH OF LIFE

Atharva-Veda

Leader: Praise to the Breath of Life, for the whole universe obeys you who is the Lord of all. On you all things are based.

All: Praise to you, O Breath of Life.

Leader: Praise to you who pours the rain, lights the sky with lightening and claps the thunder.

All: Praise to you, O Breath of Life.

Leader: Praise to you, O Breath of Life, who calls plants to life and seasons into being.

All: Praise to you, O Breath of Life.

Leader: Rained upon by you, O Breath of Life, the plants give voice, "You have prolonged for us our life and given us fragrance."

All: Praise to you, O Breath of Life.

Leader: Praise to you, O Breath of Life, when you come and when you go. Praise to you when standing still and when sitting.

All: Praise to you, O Breath of Life.

Leader: Praise to you, O Breath of Life, you hold your creatures as a father holds his beloved child.

All: Praise to you, O Breath of Life.

Leader: The Breath of Life some call the wind; again some call the breeze. The Breath of Life is sun and moon. In the Breath of Life is what is past and what is yet to be. Praise to you,

O Breath of Life, on you all things are based.

🦋 All: Praise to you, O Breath of Life.

Leader: Praise to you, O Breath of Life, you gave birth to the whole world. You rule all births and all moving things. You rule todays, tomorrows, days and nights.

Leader: The Breath of Life: Stand by us.

🦋 All: Praise to you, O Breath of Life.

Many expressions of truth flow from Brahma who Hindus believe to be the one, unifying, omnipotent creating God whose breath gives life to the universe.

☪*

FROM BEFORE THE WORLD BEGAN AND AFTER THE END OF ETERNITY

Alison Newall, Iona Community

Opening Responses

Leader: From before the world began
and after the end of eternity,
You are God.

From the sea bursting out of its womb

to the wind ceasing from its chase,
You are God.

In the constancy of created things
and in their fickleness,
You are God.

In the vastness of the universe
and the forgotten corner of our hearts,
You are God.

All: You are our God and we bless you.

Song

Psalm or Reading Concerning Creation

Confession

Leader: O God,
             your fertile earth is slowly being stripped
             of its riches.

All: Open our eyes to see.

Leader: O God, your living waters are slowly being choked
             with chemicals.

All: Open our eyes to see.

Leader: O God, your clear air is slowly being filled

                        with pollutants.

❦ All: Open our eyes to see.

   Leader: O God, your creatures are slowly dying
                and your people are suffering.

❦ All: Open our eyes to see.

   Leader: God, our Maker,
                so move us by the wonder of your creation,

❦ All: That we repent and care more deeply.

   Leader: So move us to grieve the loss of life,

❦ All: That we learn to cherish and protect your world.

Chant (During which there will be an action in which we commit ourselves to caring for God's earth and celebrate its goodness.)

Prayer of Thanksgiving/Intercession

Song

Closing Response

   Leader: This we know, the earth does not belong to us,

❦ All: We belong to the earth.

   Leader: This we know, all things are connected,

❦ All: Like the blood that unites one family.

   Leader: This we know, we did not weave the web of life,

❦ All: We are merely a strand in it.

Leader: Let us give thanks for the gift of creation,
All: Let us give thanks that all things
            hold together in our creator God.

Blessing

Leader: Bless us, O God,
            the moon that is above us,
            the earth that is beneath us,
            the friends who are around us,
            your image deep within us.
All: Amen.

In 1938, George MacLeod, a Scottish Presbyterian cleric, began rebuilding the Abbey on Iona, which had long been in ruins. He wanted the Iona Community to be a sign of the rebuilding of the common life of the church in the world. This, for him, included breaking down the barriers between prayer and politics and between the religious and the secular. His quest for the healing of the earth is evident in this liturgy. It can be used at any time during the day but is most appropriate in an outside setting in the quietness of evening after the fever of the day is hushed.

C*

EARTH AND ALL THE STARS —
AN AGAPE LITURGY

Anne Rowthorn

*The theme may be introduced and subjects of special concern
or thanksgiving suggested.*

The Ministry of Word and Prayer

Leader: In the name of God: Creator, Redeemer, and Giver of life.
Amen.

Grace to you and peace
from God our Creator,
the love at our beginning,
and without end,
in our midst and with us.

All: God is with us, here we find new life.
Leader: Let us give thanks
for the coming of God's reign of justice and love.
Jesus Christ is good news for the poor,
release for the captives,
recovery of sight for the blind
and liberty for those who are oppressed.

Canticle or Other Psalm or Canticle

Leader: O give thanks to our God who is good:

🍂 **All:**   whose love endures for ever.

Leader: You sun and moon, you stars of the southern sky,
you northern lights and midnight sun:

🍂 **All:**   give to God thanks and praise.

Leader: Sunrise and sunset, night and day:

🍂 **All:**   give to God thanks and praise.

Leader: All mountains and valleys, grassland and wood,
glacier, avalanche, mist, and snow:

🍂 **All:**   give to God thanks and praise.

Leader: Pine trees and palms, mosses and ferns:

🍂 **All:**   give to God thanks and praise.

Leader: Dolphins and whale, sea lion and crab,
coral, anemone, snail, and shrimp:

🍂 **All:**   give to God thanks and praise.

Leader: Rabbits and cattle, moths and dogs,
bee and sparrow, seagull, and hawk:

🍂 **All:**   give to God thanks and praise.

Leader: You first peoples of our lands,
all who inhabit the long white cloud:

🍂 **All:**   give to God thanks and praise.

Leader: All you saints and martyrs of Planet Earth:

🍂 **All:**   give to God thanks and praise.

Leader: All people everywhere:

🍂 **All:**   Let us give God our thanks and our praise.

A Form of Penitence

Leader: O God, as we join together in this agape, we seek your

presence. Speak to us, we pray, with the voice of your
loving spirit.

All: If our lives have become shallow, deepen them;
If our principles have become shabby, repair them.

If our ideals have become tarnished, restore them;
If our hopes have become faded, revive them.
If our loyalties have grown dim, brighten them;
If our values have become confused, clarify them.

If our purposes have grown blurred, sharpen them;
If our horizons have become narrowed, widen them.

Make us worthy instruments of your will,
And help us to live the words we pray. Amen.

Leader: God brings us new life,
the Holy One forgives and redeems us.
Let us take hold of this forgiveness
and live our lives in the spirit of
the Creator God of all the Earth.

Readings

Sermon, Meditation, or Shared Reflection

Creation Covenant (together)

All: We covenant this day with all creation,
with what was and is to be;
with every living creature,
those that sustain us, and those we sustain;

with all that moves upon the earth and the earth itself;
with all that lives in the water and with the water itself;
with all that flies through the air, and the air itself.

We confess that our own kind
has put all creation at risk.

We mark our covenant by the rainbow
as our pledge never again
to destroy creation through our greed,
our negligence,
our selfishness, and our sins.

We remember we are earth
and to earth we will return.

The Prayers of the People
(your choice or the form which follows)
Silence may be kept.

Leader: Loving God of land and sea, starry sky and infinite space,
we thank you for your gifts of creation.

All: The heavens tell of your glory.

Leader: We pray for our land, its beauty and its resources.

All: For the rich heritage we enjoy.

Leader: We pray for those who make decisions about the resources
of the earth.

All: That they may use your gifts responsibly.

Leader: For those who till the land and fish the depths, for those
who work in commerce, banking, and industry.

❦ All: That all may enjoy the fruits of their labors
and marvel at your creation.

Leader: For artists, scientists, and visionaries.

❦ All: That through their work we may see creation afresh.

(silence)

Leader: We thank you for giving us life

❦ All: For all who enrich our experience.

Leader: We pray for all who through the actions of others
are deprived of fullness of life.

❦ All: Holy God, stand with them.

Leader: For those in politics, medical science, social and relief
work, for those who teach and care for children
and the elderly.

❦ All: For all who seek to bring life to others.

(silence)

Leader: We remember all the martyrs of the earth who gave their
lives for the sake of peace and justice in this and every land.

❦ All: May we learn from their courageous acts.

(silence)

Leader: We thank you that you have called us
to celebrate your creation.

❦ All: Give us reverence for all life in your world.

Leader: We thank you for your redeeming love;

❦ All: May your word strengthen us to love as you love us.

Leader: Holy God, creator of the universe, bring us new life.

❦ All: Jesus, Redeemer, renew us.

Leader: Holy Spirit, strengthen and guide us.

The Leader concludes with an appropriate collect or one or more of the following:

God of peace,
let us your people know,
that at the heart of turbulence
there is an inner calm that comes
from faith in you.
Keep us from being content with things as they are,
that from this central peace
there may come a creative compassion,
a thirst for justice,
and a willingness to give of ourselves
in the spirit of Christ. Amen.

God, you shape our dreams.
As we put our trust in you
may your hopes and desires be ours,
and we your expectant people. Amen.

Blessed are you,
God of growth and discovery;
yours is the inspiration
that has altered and changed our lives;
yours is the power that has brought us
to new dangers and opportunities.
Guide us in your holy creation,
to walk through this world,
watching and learning,

loving and trusting,
until the coming of your reign. Amen.

The Ministry of Agape

The Peace (all standing)

Leader: The peace of God is with you.
❦ Response: In God's justice is our peace.
Leader: God calls us to live in unity.
❦ Response: We seek to live in the Spirit of Christ.
Leader: The peace of Christ be always with you.
❦ Response: And also with you.

The peace is exchanged among the people according to local custom.

Offering (together)

❦ All: With these signs and symbols from your creation, we offer
             ourselves to you, Holy God, creator of the universe. We
             bring in our eyes the waters of the rivers, the shine of the
             fish, the shade of the trees, the dew of the night, the sur
             prise of the hunt, the dance of the winds, the silver moon.
             We bring the world in our eyes.

*Offerings from creation are laid on the table. Each person brings his and her gift.
If the group is small, a word or phrase might be said as each gift is put in place.
For a larger group, hymns may be sung as the gifts are brought up.*

Introduction to the Agape *(leader)*

Jesus loved his own, and loved them to the very end. He knew that the plan to kill him was to be carried out. Now he gives the great law of his message: to love as he has loved. And he leaves a sign of his love here among human beings, in this agape.

The Christian life is a sharing in the joyous banquet of the reign of God. Every time the Christian community shares the common meal of bread and wine it celebrates the victory of Jesus on the cross, his risen presence, and the promise of his coming reign.

As we meet together to share this meal, may it express our love for one another and point us beyond ourselves in loving service in society. May it bind us together in solidarity as together we work for the peace of the world, and the healing of God's creation.

We believe in the love, mercy, and righteousness of God and ask for grace to begin anew.

May Christ be present as we share this meal so that we may share in his life. May Christ renew us and our community so that we may be signs of Christ's reign in the world.

Lord's Prayer

Leader: As Christ taught us, we now pray:

All: God our Creator, Holy one in heaven,
          may your day dawn upon us,
          may your will be done here,
          as in heaven.
          Feed us today, and forgive us,
          as we forgive each other.
          Do not forsake us at the test,
          but deliver us from evil.
          For the glory, the power, and the sovereignty are yours,
          now and forever. Amen.

Over the bread the leader says:

Leader: Blessed are you, Holy God, Ruler of the universe, for you
             bring forth bread from the earth. As grain scattered upon
             the earth is gathered into one loaf, so you gather your
             loved ones in every place into the reign of your son. To
             you be glory and power. Amen.

*The bread is then passed around the circle with each member giving a piece to
his/her neighbor with the words:*

          The bread of life and community.

Holding up the wine, the leader says:

Leader: Blessed are you, Holy God, Ruler of the universe. You create the fruit of the vine and you refresh us with the cup of salvation. Glory to you for ever and ever. Amen.

The cup is then passed around the circle with each person saying to his/her neighbor:

The cup of hope and peace.

Thanksgiving (together)

Holy and ever-living God,
we thank you for feeding us
through the spiritual food
of this agape and the nurture of this community.
We thank you for assuring us that we are living members of
the Body of Christ, destined to share in your eternal
realm. Amen.

Closing Prayer

Leader: Our liturgy is now completed. May our gracious God who broke Pharaoh's yoke and raised Jesus from the dead, forever shatter all fetters of oppression, and hasten the day when war and injustice will be no more and the earth once again be beautiful and whole. May Jesus bring redemption to all humanity — freed from violence and from wrong, united in eternal covenant and community.

❧ All: Let us now go forth into the world,
     planting seeds of hope, justice, and liberation,
     rejoicing in the power of the Spirit.
     Thanks be to God.

This is an agape (love feast), inspired by both the Jewish Passover seder liturgy and the creation liturgy of the Anglican Church of the Province of New Zealand. It was developed by Anne Rowthorn along with members of Witness for Disarmament, an interfaith peace and justice action group formed to protest the proliferation of nuclear weapons and particularly the building of nuclear submarines at a shipyard in eastern Connecticut. Here it has been adapted as a creation liturgy that can be used for a variety of occasions.

☪*

Chapter 5

BLESSINGS

Ultimately, the decision to save the environment must come form the human heart. The key point is a call for a genuine sense of universal responsibility that is based on love, compassion, and clear awareness.

— The Dalai Lama
Humanity and Ecology

PEACE OF THE RUNNING WAVE

Celtic Oral Tradition

Deep peace of the Running Wave to you.
Deep peace of the Flowing Air to you.
Deep peace of the Quiet Earth to you.
Deep peace of the Shining Stars to you.
Deep peace of the Son of Peace to you.

This blessing comes from the Celtic tradition, the indigenous Christianity of the British Isles which flourished mainly in Ireland and Scotland from the years 400–1000. The Celts had the conviction that God was present throughout all of creation — in the physical elements of earth, rocks, and water. God was in the animals and trees, in brooks and ponds; God was in the gentle winds and the rushing storms, in the stars and the depths of the oceans.

☾*

MAY THE AXE BE FAR AWAY FROM YOU

Atharva-Veda

May the axe be far away from you;
May the fire be far away from you;
May there be rain without storm.

God of the trees, may you be blessed;
God of the trees, may I be blessed.

People pray according to the ways they perceive the world and the elements of their worlds become the substance of their prayers. Thus in this prayer from the Atharva-Veda we have fire, rain, storms, and trees along with the plea that the axe — representing the evil forces of the universe — "be far away from you."

C*

THE BLESSING OF LIGHT

Author Unknown

May the blessing of light be on you,
    light without and light within.

May the blessed sunlight shine upon you
    and warm your heart
    till it glows like a great fire
    and strangers may warm themselves
    as well as friends.

And may the light shine out of the eyes of you,
    like a candle set

in the window of a house,
bidding the wanderer to come in
out of the storm.

May the blessing of rain be on you,
to beat upon your spirit
and wash it fair and clean;
and leave there many a shining pool
where the blue of heavens shines,
and sometimes a star.

May the blessing of the earth be upon you,
the great round earth.

May you ever have a kindly greeting for people
as you're going along the roads.

And now may God bless you,
and bless you kindly.

This Irish prayer may be of recent origin written in an ancient Celtic style. The mention of candles in the window of the house suggests this. It is a prayer of hospitality, bidding the blessings of light, sunshine, rain, and the good earth and it only asks us in return to have a kindly greeting for people as we are "going along the roads."

C*

BLESSINGS OF HEAVEN

Celtic Oral Tradition

May God Almighty bless you,
blessings of heaven above
blessings of the deep lying below
blessings of the breasts and womb
blessings of the grain and flowers
blessings of the eternal mountains
bounty of the everlasting hills,
be bound with you and go with you,
in the name of the Father, Son, and Holy Spirit.

"Blessings of Heaven" is a practical example of what happened with the Christianization of the Celtic religion. The Celts, the indigenous people of Ireland, Scotland, and Wales, already had a highly developed pantheistic religion when Christianity was brought to the islands. With its arrival, the Celts did not reject their natural theology but grafted Christianity on to it. Thus, in the first line of this ancient prayer, "God" has been changed to "Almighty God" and "Father, Son, and Holy Spirit" have been added to the last line. The result is a pleasing blending of both traditions.

C*

THE WHITE SUN HAS SUNK
BEYOND THE HILLS

Wang Tsu-haun

The white sun has sunk behind the hills.
The yellow river is pouring into the sea.
To see still further into the horizon,
Let us go up one more story!

The enormous appeal of Chinese landscape poetry to the western ear — as illustrated by Wang Tsu-haun's verse — is that it evokes an intimate expression of personal feeling. There is an immediacy about it that reaches out to touch the core of our being. This effect is achieved through the poet's deep penetration into both the particular and the present. The yellow river is pouring into the sea right now, not yesterday, not tomorrow but right now.

☾*

CREATOR SPIRIT

The Brothers of Weston Priory

Creator Spirit,
mighty wind of God,

You brood over our lives,
and speak new life into our chaos.
You set Your Sabbath apart for Your service.

Your Sabbath
celebrates the flowering of creation,
the wedding of our hopes
to Your divine yearning.
In the light of your holy Sabbath,
each day is holy;
in the overflowing of Sabbath joy,
each moment is sacred.

As we read in the story of creation:
"Now the whole universe
— sky, earth, and all their array
— was completed.
With the seventh day,
God enjoyed rest from the labor of creation.
Then God blessed the seventh day,
and called it holy."

Overshadow us now
with your beauty and your joy,
that our world may know
a Sabbath of wholeness and peace,
today and forever.

Every year thousands of people visit the Weston Priory on a hilltop at the edge of the Green Mountains in southern Vermont. The singing monks have drawn such a following by the holiness of their living, their courageous and compassionate actions for justice and world peace, and by the depth of their prayer.

☾*

MAY THE ICE BLANKET SPREAD OUT

Zuñi Prayer

Following whatever roads the rainmakers mark out:
May the ice blanket spread out,
May the ice blanket cover the country;
All over the land.
May the flesh of our Earth Mother
Crack open from the cold;
That your thoughts may bend to this,
That your words may be to this end.
For this with prayers I send you forth.

Nothing is known about the Zuñi poet who wrote "May the Ice Blanket Spread Out" or of the ethnologist who discovered it. Like so many of life's blessings, this beautiful prayer is a precious gift whose source is hidden from us.

☾*

PEACE BE TO EARTH AND AIRY SPACE

Atharva-Veda

Peace be to earth and airy space.
Peace be to heaven, peace to the waters,
Peace to the plants and peace to the trees.
May all the powers grant us peace.
By this invocation of peace may peace be diffused.
By this invocation of peace may peace bring peace.
With this peace the dreadful we now appease,
With this peace all evil we now appease,
With this peace the cruel we now appease,
So that peace may prevail.
May everything be peaceful.

The latest of the four Vedas is the Atharva-Veda, full of cosmological hymns and chants. The Atharva-Veda assumes an all-powerful god and in places suggests that this god needs to be placated. This prayer also brings to mind the yin/yang idea that all life is an eternal interplay between opposing forces — peaceful/dreadful, good/evil, kindness/cruelty. Amidst these tensions, this Veda offers a prayer that "peace may prevail."

☾*

AS THE EARTH KEEPS TURNING

World Council of Churches

As the earth keeps turning, hurtling through space;
and night falls and day breaks from land to land;
Let us remember people — waking, sleeping, being born and dying —
of one world and of one humanity. Let us go from here in peace.

This blessing, part of a larger evening litany, was used at the Nairobi Assembly of the World Council of Churches in 1975.

☾*

MAY THERE BE PEACE IN THE SKY

Atharva-Veda

Supreme God,
Let there be peace in the sky and in the atmosphere,
peace in the plant world and in the forests.
Let the cosmic powers be peaceful.
Let the Holy One be peaceful.
Let there be undiluted and fulfilling peace everywhere.

Hinduism is a religion of incredible complexity and variety, yet its earliest prayers are remarkably simple and direct, as illustrated by this short prayer, taken from the Atharva-Veda.

☾*

BENEDICTIO

Edward Abbey

May your trails be crooked, winding, lonesome, dangerous,
    leading to the most amazing views.
May your mountains rise into and above the clouds.
May your rivers flow without end,
    meandering through pastoral valleys tinkling with bells, past
    temples and castles and poets' towers into a dark primeval forest
    where tigers belch and monkeys howl,
    through miasmal and mysterious swamps and down into a desert of
    red rock, blue mesas, domes and pinnacles and grottoes of endless
    stone, and down again into a deep vast ancient unknown chasm
    where bars of sunlight blaze on profiled cliffs,
    where deer walk across the white sand beaches,
    where storms come and go as lightning clangs upon the high crags,
    where something strange and more beautiful and more full of
    wonder than your deepest dreams waits for you —
    beyond the turning of the canyon walls.
        So long.

To his detractors Edward Abbey (1927–1998) was an "eco-terrorist" whose writings encouraged the radical actions of the environmental action group, EarthFirst! To his friends, he was a man of humor, warmth, and passion. Concerning the environment, Abbey once said, "It's not enough to understand the natural world. The point is to defend it." Abbey was best known for his novels — among them: The Monkey Wrench Gang, Heyduke Lives!, Brave Cowboy, Fire on the Mountain — *and for his prose — especially* Desert Solitaire. *He rarely published his poems and kept most of them in personal journals. "Benedicito" (bless-ing) is one of his last, thus the "So long" at the end is both appropriate and poignant.*

☾*

MAY THE ROAD RISE TO MEET YOU

Celtic Oral Tradition

May the road rise to meet you.
May the wind always be at your back.
May the sun shine warm upon your face.
May the rains fall softly upon your fields
until we meet again.

Celts have always been a people on the move — from their original home around the Black Sea in 1000 B.C.E.., to central Europe and the Pyrenees in 600 B.C.E., and finally westward to Ireland and the Scottish islands. Pilgrimage was an outward expression of an inner voyage toward deeper faith and greater holiness. This blessing is for all of us traveling that road.

What we call the beginning is often the end
And to make an end is to make a beginning.
The end is where we start from.

— T. S. Eliot
Four Quartets

LIST OF CONTRIBUTORS

CONTRIBUTIONS FROM OTHER SOURCES

Vedas

Author Unknown

Blessing of Light, The   302
Great Blue Heron, The   156
Litany of Sorrow, A   235
Litany of Thanksgiving for the Americas, A   241
We Live in Relation to All Things   244

Sacred Writings

Deuteronomy 8
Isaiah 65
Isaiah 11
Job 12
Koran, The
Psalm 104
Sirach 43
Song of the Three Young Men
   (Apocrypha)
Tao Te Ching

Land of Flowing Streams, A   55
New Heaven and A New Earth, A   114
Peaceful Earth, The   87
Ask the Animals   192
Praise Belongs to God   16
You Spread out the Heavens   110
Holy One Has Made All Things, The   27

Creation's Song of Praise   268
Heaven and Earth Abide   40

Contemporary Religious Groups

Brothers of Weston Priory, The
Central Conference of American Rabbis

Free Church of Berkeley

Iona Community

Kurama Temple
Metropolitan Tryphon
New York Board of Rabbis

Creator Spirit   305
As You Leave Eden behind You   102
Divine Voice Sings through All Creation, A   267
Architect of the Worlds   144
For Purity of Air and Water   127
Restore Our Earth Household   255
From before the World Began and
   after the End of Eternity   284
In the Beginning, God Made the World   261
Let the Light Fall Warm and Red on the Rock   245
Prayer of Love, Light, and Power   119
Praise of God's Creation in Chants and Echoes   271
Prayer of Adoration for Creation, A   123

Cultural Traditions

PERMISSION ACKNOWLEDGMENTS

Grateful acknowledgment is given to the following publishers and copyright holders for permission to reprint the quotations in *Earth and All the Stars*. Every effort has been made to contact all rights holders of the material in *Earth and All the Stars*. The editor promises to correct any omissions or mistakes in acknowledgments in future editions.

INTRODUCTION

From Ki no Tsurayuki, "Kanajo, the Japanese Preface" in *Kokinshu: A Collection of Poems Ancient and Modern*, ed. Laura Rasplica Rodd (Princeton, N.J.: Princeton University Press, 1984), 35.

From David Tracy, *On Naming the Present* (Maryknoll, N.Y.: Orbis Books, 1994), 137.

CHAPTER 1: CREATION STORIES AND REFLECTIONS

Warriors of the Rainbow: From William Willoya and Vinson Brown, *Warriors of the Rainbow: Strange and Prophetic Dreams of the Indian Peoples* (Happycamp, Calif.: Naturegraph Publishers, 1962) 1992, 15. Reprinted by permission.

The Golden Womb of the Sun: From "To an Unknown God" (original title), Mandala X, Song 121, a song of the Rig-Veda, in *The Golden Womb of the Sun*, 2nd ed., ed. P. Lal (Calcutta, India: Writers Workshop, 1970). Last line added by Anne Rowthorn. Copyright © by Writers Workshop, Calcutta, India. Reprinted by permission.

The Creation: From James Weldon Johnson, *God's Trombones* (New York: Viking, 1927), 17. Copyright © 1927 by The Viking Press, Inc., renewed © by Grace Nail Johnson. Used by permission of Viking Penguin, a division of Penguin Putnam, Inc.

Creation Story: A Retelling: Moyra Caldecott, From a service bulletin for the Creation Festival Liturgy, Coventry Cathedral (Coventry, England, October 9, 1988), 11–17. Used by permission of the International Consultancy on Religion, Education, and Culture (IOREC).

Praise Belongs to God: From *The Koran Interpreted*, trans. Arthur J. Arberry (New York: Macmillan, 1988), vol. 1:149, 267, 287; vol. II: 138, 139. Reprinted with the permission of Simon & Schuster from *The Koran Interpreted* translated by A. J. Arberry, copyright © 1955 by George Allen and Unwin, Ltd.

Otokahekagapi: *Otokahekagapi (First Beginnings): Sioux Creation Story*, transcribed from oral tradition, translated and illustrated by Thomas E. Simms with Lakota translations by Ben Black Bear Jr. (Chamberlain, S.D.: Tipi Press, 1987).

Well I'll Be: Source unknown. Reported in *Christian Spirituality* (Winter, 1995). Reprinted by permission of Matthew Fox.

Before God Created the World: From Japji Sahib and Rag Gaur Bairagan, "Guru Granth Sahib," *The Sikh Statement on Nature* (Gland, Switzerland: World Wide Fund for Nature), 464. "Sikh Statement on Nature." Date and copyright information unknown.

Entering the Twenty-First Century: From Thich Nhat Hanh, *Peace Is Every Step,* ed. Arnold Kotler (New York: Bantam Books, 1992), 134. Used by permission of Thich Nhat Hanh.

The Holy One Has Made All Things: From Sirach 43, "The Apocryphal Deuterocanonical Books of the Old Testament," *The Holy Bible, New Revised Standard Version* (New York: Oxford University Press, 1989). Copyright © 1989 by Division of Christian Education of the National Council of the Churches of Christ in the United States of America. Used by permission.

Silence: From Peter Gold, *Altar of the Earth: The Life, Land, and Spirit of Tibet* (Ithaca, N.Y.: Snow Lion Publications, 1987), 40. Used by permission.

Toward the Bosom of the Newly Rising Sun: From *Korean Poetry Today,* ed. Jaihiun J. Kim (Seoul, Korea: Hanshin Publishing Co., 1987), 126–127. Translation copyright © 1987 by Jaihiun J. Kim.

Learn From the Pine: From *The Essential Haiku,* ed. and trans. Robert Hass (Hopewell, N.J. Ecco Press, 1994), 233–237 passim. Selection and translation copyright © 1994 by Robert Hass. Reprinted by permission of The Ecco Press.

I Am the Sunrise: From Matthew Fox, et al., "The I Am Workshop Poem" in *Christian Spirituality* (Winter, 1995), 23–25. Abbreviated and adapted. The Christian spirituality tradition is being taught in a Master's Degree program and a Doctor of Ministry program at the University of Christian Spirituality and Naropa Institute in Oakland, CA, Matthew Fox, President. 510-835-4827, e-mail ucs@csnet.org.

Heaven and Earth Abide: Extracts from the *The Way of Ways: Tao,* Vol. 33, no.7, trans. Herrymon Maurer (Princeton: N.J.: Fellowship in Prayer, 1982), chapters 7, 8, 19, 22, 25, 29, 35, 38, 41, 57, 64, 72, 78, and 81. Copyright © 1982 by Herrymon Maurer. Used by permission of Helen S. Maurer.

God of the Earth, Our Mother, Make a Wide World for Us: From "Hymn to the Earth" Atharva-Veda XII in *Hymns from the Vedas: Original Text and English Translation,* ed. Abinash Chandra Bose (Bombay: Asia Publishing House, 1966). Abridged and adapted by Anne Rowthorn.

Any Fool Can Destroy Trees: From John Muir, *Our National Parks* (Boston: Houghton Mifflin, 1909), 303–305.

Canticle of Brother Sun: From *The Writings of St. Francis of Assisi,* ed. Benen Fahy (Chicago: Franciscan Herald Press, 1964), 130–131. Adapted and used by permission of Franciscan Press, Quincy, Ill.

A Land of Flowing Streams: From Deuteronomy 8:7–15, *The New Jerusalem Bible* (New York: Doubleday, 1999). Excerpt from *The New Jerusalem Bible,* copyright © 1985 by Darton, Longman and Todd Ltd. and Doubleday, a division of Random House, Inc. Reprinted by permission.

Looking Deeply: From Thich Nhat Hanh, *Peace Is Every Step* (New York: Bantam Books, 1992), 104–106 passim. Adapted. Used by permission of Thich Nhat Hanh.

To Whom Does the Earth Belong?: From Al-Hafiz B. A. Masri, "Islam and Ecology," in *Islam and Ecology,* ed. Fazlun M. Khalid with Joanne O'Brien (London: Cassell Publishers, 1992), 1–2, 5–7, 21–22, passim. © Cassell plc, with permission.

On Genesis: From Kwansik Kim in *Korean Poetry Today,* ed. Jaihiun J. Kim (Seoul, Korea: Hanshin Publishing, 1987), 257–258. Translation copyright © 1987 by Jaihiun J. Kim.

Nature We See: From Guru Nānak, "Guru Granth Sahib," *The Sikh Statement on Nature* (Gland, Switzerland: World Wide Fund for Nature), 464.

Every Part of the Earth Is Sacred: Letter from Chief Seattle to President Polk, 1812, quoted in *The Power of Myth* by

Joseph Campbell with Bill Moyers (New York: Doubleday, 1988), 34–35.

Touch the Earth: From Luther Standing Bear, *Land of the Spotted Eagle* (Boston: Houghton Mifflin, 1933), 192–197.

A Revolution for Animals, Rivers, Lakes, and Trees: From Ernesto Cardenal, "New Ecology" (original title), trans. Dinah Livingstone, *Nicaragua New Time* (London: The Journeyman Press, 1988), 68–70. Used by permission of Pluto Press.

And God Became an Indian: From José Gómez, *Pax Christi News* (Hartford, Conn. Chapter, March 1992).

Mindful Verses: From Thich Nhat Hanh, "Look Deeply and Smile," in *Buddhism and Ecology*, ed. Martine Batchelor and Kerry Brown (London: Cassell Publishers, Ltd., 1992), 104–107. Used by permission of Thich Nhat Hanh.

Nature: From Ralph Waldo Emerson, "Nature," in *Nature: Addresses and Lectures* (Boston: Houghton Mifflin, n.d.), 103. Edited and abridged for this publication by Anne Rowthorn.

I Dream: From Mainak Bhusan Banerjee, in *Children's State of the Planet Handbook* (Hilversum, Netherlands: Peace Child International, 1992). Copyright © 1992 by Peace Child International and the *Children's State of the Planet Handbook.* Used by permission.

The Peaceful Earth: From Isaiah 11:6–9, *The New Jerusalem Bible* (New York: Doubleday, 1999). Copyright © 1985 by Darton, Longman and Todd Ltd. and Doubleday, a division of Random House, Inc. Reprinted by permission.

Into the Mountains: From John Muir, *The Yosemite* (Boston: Houghton Mifflin, 1912) and John Muir, *Our National Parks* (Boston: Houghton Mifflin, 1909).

The Earth My Dream: From Margaret Uyanga, *Children's State of the Planet Handbook* (Hilversum, Netherlands: Peace Child International, 1992). Copyright © 1992 by Peace Child International and the *Children's State of the Planet Handbook.* Used by permission.

The Once and Future Planet: From Ellen, "A Passing Thing," in *Children's State of the Planet Handbook* (Hilversum, Netherlands: Peace Child International, 1992). Copyright © 1992 by Peace Child International and the *Children's State of the Planet Handbook.* Used by permission.

Walking So That All Beings May Be Peaceful: From Thich Nhat Hanh, *A Guide to Walking Meditation*, trans. Jenny Hoang and Anh Huong, ed. Robert Aitkin and Joseph Bobro Nyak (New York: Fellowship of Reconciliation, 1985). Used by permission of Thich Nhat Hanh.

Take One Last Look: From Adita Charda, *Rescue Mission: Planet Earth: A Children's Edition of Agenda 21* (London: Kingfisher Books, Earth Day, 1994), 53.

Death: From Aleksandra Warzecka, *Rescue Mission: Planet Earth, A Children's Edition of Agenda 21* (London: Kingfisher Books, Earth Day, 1994), 11.

Widening Our Circle of Compassion: From Albert Einstein, quoted in "Participants Guide," *One God, Family, Earth: Responding to the Gifts of God's Creation* (New York: Episcopal Church Center, 1994).

Thinking Globally: A Universal Task: From The Dalai Lama, "Thinking Globally: A Universal Task," reprinted in *The Wisdom and Teachings of the Dalai Lama*, ed. Matthew E. Bunson (New York: Penguin, 1997), 208–209.

Walden: From Henry David Thoreau, *Walden* (Boston, 1853). Reprinted in Masters of American Literature, vol. 1, ed. Henry A. Pochman and Gay W. Allen (New York: Macmillan, 1949).

When the Last Leaf Falls: From Tove, *Children's State of the Planet Handbook* (Hilversum, Netherlands: Peace Child

20

International, 1992). Copyright © 1992 by Peace Child International and *Children's State of the Planet Handbook.* Used by permission.

As You Leave Eden behind You: From *Gates of Prayer: The New Union Prayerbook* (New York: Central Conference of American Rabbis, 1975), 656–657.

The Golden Thread: From William Willoya and Vinson Brown, *Warriors of the Rainbow: Strange and Prophetic Dreams of the Indian Peoples* (Happy Camp, Calif.: Naturegraph Publishers, Inc., 1962), 1992. Copyright © 1962 by Naturegraph Publishers: Happycamp, California. Used with permission.

The Glory of the Forest Meadow Is the Lily: From John Muir, *My First Summer in the Sierra* (Boston: Houghton Mifflin, 1911).

You Spread out the Heavens: From Psalm 104:1–23, 25–31, *Book of Common Prayer* (Episcopal Church) (New York: The Church Hymnal Corporation, 1977).

A New Heaven and a New Earth: From Isaiah 65:17–25, *The Holy Bible, New Revised Standard Version* (New York: Oxford University Press, 1989). Copyright © 1989 by New Revised Standard Version Bible Division of Christian Education of the National Council of the Churches of Christ in the United States of America. Used by permission.

CHAPTER 2: PRAYERS

Prayer of Love, Light, and Power: From *Prayer for the Happiness to the Sonten of Kuramayama* (original title) (Kyoto, Japan: Kurama Temple). Used by permission of Kurama Temple.

Opening the Gate of the Clouds: From Li Po, *The Four Seasons of T'ang Poetry*, ed. John C. H. Wu (Rutland,Vt. and Tokyo, Japan: Charles E. Tuttle Co., 1972). Used by permission of Charles E. Tuttle, Inc., of Boston, Massachusetts and Tokyo, Japan.

The Morning Is Yours: From Celtic prayer, source unknown. Quoted in *Tides and Seasons* by David Adam (London: Triangle/SPCK, 1989), 9.

A Prayer Adoration for Creation: From *A Treasury of Jewish Inspiration*, ed. Philip Goodman (New York: New York Board of Rabbis, 1962). Adapted.

The Hand Transforms Nature: From Jaci C. Maraschin in *"And God Saw That It Was Good…" A Brazilian Liturgy of Creation*, by Ernesto Cardoso and Marcos Gianelli (Geneva: World Council of Churches, 1989). From D. Pedro Casaldaliga and Milton Nascimento, "Missa dos Quilombros," *A Brazilian Liturgy of Creation*, by Ernesto Cardoso and Marcos Gianelli (Geneva: World Council of Churches, 1989).

In Praise of Creation: From Fyodor Dostoyevsky, *The Brothers Karamazov*, quoted in *Fellowship in Prayer* (Princeton: N.J.: Fellowship in Prayer, 1995).

For Purity of Air and Water: From *The Covenant of Peace: A Liberation Prayer Book* (Free Church of Berkeley), ed. John Pairman Brown and Richard L. York (New York: Morehouse-Barlow, 1971), 43. Copyrght © 1971 The Free Church of Berkeley. Used by permission.

The Web of Life: From Anne Rowthorn, inspired by "An Earth Charter," Interfaith Coordinating Committee on Religion and the Earth (ICCRE).

Thanksgiving Day: From Anne Rowthorn, "Thanksgiving Day." Copyright © 1994 by Anne Rowthorn.

For the Hardest Places on Earth: Quoted in *With All God's People: The Ecumenical Prayer Cycle* (Geneva, Switzerland;

World Council of Churches, 2nd ed., 1990), 342. Original source unknown.

O Creating God Who Spreads the Earth, Forgive Us and Love Us. From "To Varuna" (original title), Mandala V, Song 85, a song from the Rig-Veda, in *The Golden Womb of the Sun*, 2nd ed., ed. by P. Lal. (Calcutta, India: Writers Workshop, 1970), 27–28. Copyright © 1970 by Writers Workshop, Calcutta, India. Used by permission.

When Spring Comes: Author unknown. From Ruth L. Bunzel in "Introduction to Zuñi Ceremonialism," *Forty-seventh Annual Report of the Bureau of Zuñi American Ethnology*, 1929-1930 (Washington, D.C., 1932), 484.

I Believe: Copyright © 1995 by Anne Rowthorn.

The Rainbow Covenant: From Martin Palmer, *Lord of Creation* (Worldwide Fund for Nature/Yorkshire Television, 1987). Used by permission of Martin Palmer.

Hymn to the Earth: From "Hymn to the Earth," in the Atharva-Veda, 12.1. Paraphrase from the translation quoted by O. D. Dwivedi and B. N. Tiwari in *Environmental Crisis and Hindu Religion* (New Delhi: Gitanjali, 1987).

An Indian Prayer: From Tom White Cloud, "An Indian Prayer," a prayer on a roadside plaque, erected by the Akwesesne Mohawk Counselor Organization (Hogansburg, N.Y.: St. Regis Reservation).

O Jesus, Be the Canoe: Author unknown. From "Melanesia News," reprinted in *Morning, Noon, and Night*, compiled John Carden (London: CMS, 1976), 95.

Creating God, Your Fingers Trace: From Jeffery Rowthorn, "Creating God, Your Fingers Trace," (Carol Stream, Ill.: Hope Publishing, 1974). Copyright © 1974 by The Hymn Society. All rights reserved. Used by permission.

Architect of the Worlds: From *The Covenant of Peace: A Liberation Prayer Book* (Free Church of Berkeley), ed. by John Pairman Brown and Richard L. York (New York: Morehouse-Barlow, 1971), 42. Copyright © 1971 by The Free Church of Berkeley. Used by permission.

Covered with Frost Flowers: Author unknown. From Ruth Bunzel, "Introduction to Zuñi Ceremonialism," In *Forty-seventh Annual Report of the Bureau of Zuñi American Ethnology*, 1929–1930 (Washington, D.C., 1932), 483–484.

O God, May I Speak...: From Chiara Lubich, *Spiel mit Gott Lichen Rollen* (Munich: Neue Stadt Verlag, n.d.). Copyright by Città Editrice, Rome, Italy.

CHAPTER 3: POEMS

I Am the Wind: Amergin, *The Deer's Cry: A Treasury of Irish Religious Verse*, ed. P. Murray (Dublin: Four Courts Press, 1986), 15.

God of All: From St. Patrick, *Tides and Seasons: Modern Prayers in Celtic Tradition* by David Adam (London: Triangle/SPCK, 1989), xi. Used by permission.

The Great Blue Heron: Author unknown. From a plaque at the City Hall of Portland, Oregon.

Oh Earth, Wait for Me: From Pablo Neruda, *Poems: Pablo Neruda*, trans. Alastair Reid, ed. Nathaniel Tarn (London: Jonathan Cape, 1975). Used by permission of Jonathan Cape.

Snow Is Falling: From Boris Pasternak, *Pasternak: In the Interlude–Poems 1945–1960*, trans. Henry Kamen (London: Oxford University Press, 1962). Reprinted by permission of the Peters Fraser and Dunlop Group Limited, on behalf of © Henry Kamen.

Imagining the Divine. From Diane Ackerman. Copyright © 1999 by Diane Ackerman. Used by generous permission of the author.

Flowing along the Border of Heaven: From Li Po, *Along the Border of Heaven: Sung and Yüng Paintings from the C. C. Wang*

Family Collection (New York: The Metropolitan Museum of Art, 1983). Reprinted by permission of The Metropolitan Museum of Art.

Every Petal, Every Speck: From Liu K'O-chuang, "To the Fortune Teller" (original title), *The Penguin Book of Chinese Verse*, trans. Robert Kotewall and Norman S. Smith (Middlesex, England: Penguin Books, 1962), 52. Translation copyright © 1962 by N. L. Smith and R. H. Kotewall. Used by permission.

In the Sixth Month: From Bashō, selected haiku: first poem from *Haiku, vol. 1*, trans. by R. H. Blyth (Tokyo: Hokuseido Press, 1953), 120. Copyright © 1952, 1953. By permission of Hokuseido Press. All other poems from *The Essential Haiku: Versions of Bashō, Buson, and Issa*, ed. and trans. Robert Hass (Hopewell, N.J.: The Ecco Press, 1994), 19, 21, 26, 33, 54. Selection and translation copyright © 1994 by Robert Hass. Reprinted by permission of The Ecco Press.

The Waking: From Theodore Roethke, *The Collected Poems of Theodore Roethke* (New York: Doubleday, 1953). Copyright © 1953 by Theodore Roethke. Used by permission of Doubleday, a division of Random House, Inc.

In Hardwood Groves: From Robert Frost, *The Poetry of Robert Frost*, ed. Edward Connery Lathem. Copyright 1942, 1951, © 1962 by Robert Frost. Copyright © 1970 by Lesley Frost Ballantine. Copyright 1923, 1924, © 1969 by Henry Holt and Co., LLC. Reprinted by permission of Henry Holt and Company, LLC.

Bees: From Lo Yin, *The Penguin Book of Chinese Verse*, trans. Robert Kotewall and Norman S. Smith (Middlesex, England: Penguin Books, Ltd., 1962), 28. Translation copyright © 1962 by N. L. Smith and R. H. Kotewall. Used by permission.

Enchantments of the River: From *Paulo Gabriel, Poets of Araguaia*, ed. Rodrigues Brandao, trans. Colleen Reeks, quoted in *And God Saw That It Was Good* by Ernesto Cardoso and Marcos Gianelli (Geneva: World Council of Churches, 1989). Used by permission of the World Council of Churches.

The Chill Snow: From Yeh Pao-sung, "Hsiao-ch'a Shan Pavilion" (original title), *The Penguin Book of Chinese Verse*, trans. Robert Kotewall and Norman L. Smith (Middlesex, England: Penguin Books, Ltd., 1962), 70. Translation copyright © 1962 by N. L. Smith and R. H. Kotewall. Used by permission.

Green Leaves, White Water: First five haiku from Buson, *The Essential Haiku: Versions of Bashō, Buson, and Issa*, ed. and trans. by Robert Hass (Hopewell, N.J.: The Ecco Press, 1994), 82, 86, 104, 111, 116, 122. Selection and copyright © 1994 by Robert Hass. Reprinted by permission of The Ecco Press. The sixth haiku from Buson, *Haiku, Vol. 11*, ed. R. H. Blyth (Tokyo: Hokuseido Press, 1952), 219. Copyright © 1952, 1953. By permission of Hokuseido Press.

Friends We Shall Become: From Geoffrey Duncan, *Dare to Dream*, ed. Geoffrey Duncan (London: HarperCollins Publishers, 1995). Used by permission of HarperCollins, Ltd.

New Feet within My Garden Go: From Emily Dickinson, *The Poems of Emily Dickinson*, ed. Thomas H. Johnson (Cambridge, Mass.: Belknap Press of Harvard University, 1951, 1955). Reprinted by permission of the publishers and the Trustees of Amherst College. Copyright © 1951, 1955, 1979, 1983 by the President and Fellows of Harvard College.

A Prayer in Spring: From Robert Frost, *The Poetry of Robert Frost*, ed. Edward Connery Lathem. Copyright 1942, 1951, © 1962 by Robert Frost. Copyright © 1970 by Lesley Frost Ballantine. Copyright 1923, 1934, © 1969 by Henry Holt and Company, LLC. Reprinted by permission of Henry Holt and Company, LLC.

The Maple Grove: From Yüan Hao-wen, "Miscellaneous Poems of Mountain Life, IV" (original title), *The Penguin*

Book of Chinese Verse, trans. Robert Kotewall and Norman L. Smith (Middlesex, England: Penguin Book, Ltd., 1962), 52. Translation copyright © 1962 by N. L. Smith and Robert Kotewall. Used by permission.

Question and Answer among the Mountains: From Li Po, *The Penguin Book of Chinese Verse*, trans. Robert Kotewall and Norman S. Smith (Middlesex, England: Penguin Books, Ltd., 1962), 14. Translation copyright © 1962 by N. L. Smith and R. H. Kotewall. Used by permission.

A Single Plum Tree: From Chu Tun-ju, "To the Fortune Teller" (original title), *The Penguin Book of Chinese Verse*, trans. Robert Kotewall and Norman L. Smith (Middlesex, England: Penguin Book, Ltd., 1962), 44. Translation copyright © 1962 by N. L. Smith and R. H. Kotewall. Used by permission.

In This World: From Issa, *The Essential Haiku: Versions of Bashō, Buson and Issa*, ed. and trans. Robert Hass (Hopewell, N.J.: The Ecco Press, 1994), 158, 179, 184, 192, 196. Selection and copyright © 1994 by Robert Hass. Reprinted by permission of The Ecco Press.

Come In: From Robert Frost, *The Poetry of Robert Frost*, ed. Edward Connery Lathem. Copyright 1942, 1951, © 1962 by Robert Frost. Copyright © 1970 by Leslie Frost Ballantine. Copyright 1923, 1934, © 1969 by Henry Holt and Company LLC. Reprinted by permission of Henry Holt and Co., LLC.

Earth Song: From Don DiVecchio, *Spare Change: Massachusetts Journal of the Streets* (Cambridge, 31 December–13 January 1999). Copyright © 1988 by Don DiVecchio. Used by generous permission of Don DiVecchio.

For Two Thousand Miles: From Kao K'O-kung, "Passing Tthrough Hsin-chou," *The Penguin Book of Chinese Verse*, ed. Robert Kotewall and Norman L. Smith (Middlesex, England: Penguin Books, Ltd., 1962), 54. Translation copyright © N. L. Smith and R. H. Kotewall, 1962. Used by permission.

Ask the Animals: From Job 12:7–10, *The New Jerusalem Bible* (New York: Doubleday, 1999). Copyright © 1985 by Darton, Longman and Todd Ltd. and Doubleday, a division of Random House, Inc. Reprinted by permission.

A Quiet Temple Thick Set with Flowers: From Li Po, *The Four Seasons of T'ang Poetry*, ed. John C. H. Wu (Rutland, Vt. and Tokyo, Japan: Charles E. Tuttle, 1972). Used by permission of Charles E. Tuttle Co., Inc. of Boston, Massachusetts and Tokyo, Japan.

Lamentation of the Rocks: From Robert O'Rourke, "Rock Ritual XX: Lamentation of the Rocks" (original title), *Fellowship in Prayer* (Princeton: N.J.: Fellowship in Prayer, 1995). Used by generous permission of Robert O'Rourke.

The Little Peach Trees: From Tai Fu-ku, "In a Huai Village after the Fighting" (original title), in *The Penguin Book of Chinese Verse*, trans. Robert Kotewall and Norman S. Smith (Middlesex, England: Penguin Books, Ltd., 1962), 50. Translation copyright © 1962 by N. L. Smith and R. H. Kotewall. Used by permission.

Cape Ann: From T. S. Eliot, *Collected Poems 1909–1962* (New York: Harcourt, Brace and World, 1936). Copyright 1936 by Harcourt, Inc., copyright © 1964, 1963 by T. S. Eliot. Reprinted by permission of the publisher.

Light: From Hyonsung Kim, *Korean Poetry Today*, ed. Jaihiun J. Kim (Seoul, Korea: Hanshin Publishing Co., 1987), 108. Translation copyright © 1987 by Jaihuin J. Kim.

Journey at Dawn: From Lin Shao-chan, *The Penguin Book of Chinese Verse*, trans. Robert Kotewall and Norman S. Smith (Middlesex, England: Penguin Books, Ltd., 1962), 46. Translation copyright © 1962 by N. L. Smith and R. H. Kotewall. Used by permission.

The Waterfall: From Chang Chiu-ling (Zhang Jiuling), *A Golden Treasury of Chinese Poetry*, trans. John Turner (Hong Kong: Renditions Paperbacks, 1989), 29. Used by permission of the Research Center for Translation, Chinese

University of Hong Kong.

Moments of Rising Mist: From Chinese landscape poets of the Sung Dynasty, *Moments of Rising Mist*, ed. and trans. Amitendranath Tagore (New York: Grossman Publishers, 1973).

Nothing Gold Can Stay: From Robert Frost, *The Poetry of Robert Frost*, ed. Edward Connery Lathem. Copyright 1942, 1951, © 1962 by Robert Frost. Copyright © 1970 by Lesley Frost Ballantine. Copyright 1923, 1934, © 1969 by Henry Holt and Company LLC. Reprinted by permission of Henry Holt and Company, LLC.

Ten Thousand Things Respond to Spring Sun: From Ou-yang Hsiu. *An Introduction to Sung Poetry*, ed. Kojiro Yoshikawa, trans. Burton Watson (Cambridge, MA: Harvard University Press, 1967). Copyright © 1976 by the Harvard-Yenching Institute. Reprinted by permission of the Harvard University Press.

The First Snow of the Year: From Bashō, Shiki, Hashin, and Joso, *Japanese Haiku*, vol. 4 (Winter), trans. R. H. Blyth (Tokyo: Hokuseido Press, 1952). Copyright © 1952, 1953. Used by permission of Hokuseido Press.

Sound: From Kijo Song, *Korean Poetry Today*, ed. Jaihiun J. Kim (Seoul, Korea: Hanshin Publishing Co., 1987), 308. Translation copyright © 1987 by Jaihiun J. Kim.

Looking for a Sunset Bird in Winter: From Robert Frost, *The Poetry of Robert Frost*, ed. Edward Connery Lathem. Copyright 1942, 1951, © 1962 by Robert Frost. Copyright © 1970 by Lesley Frost Ballantine. Copyright 1923, 1934, © 1969 by Henry Holt and Company, LLC. Reprinted by permission of Henry Holt and Company, LLC.

The Far Echoes of the Tides: From Tu Hsün-hê, *The Four Seasons of T'ang Poetry*, ed. John C. H. Wu Rutland, (Vt. and Tokyo, Japan: Charles E. Tuttle Co., 1972). Used by permission of Charles E. Tuttle Co., Inc., of Boston, Massachusetts and Tokyo, Japan.

Something Greater Than Heaven: From Seuk Ho, *Korean Poetry Today*, ed. Jaihiun J. Kim (Seoul, Korea: Hanshin Publishing Co., 1987), 325. Translation copyright © 1987 by Jaihun J. Kim.

CHAPTER 4: RITES AND CELEBRATIONS

We Face East: From a service, 1492–1992: *A Celebration of Native American Survival* (Washington, D.C.: Cathedral Church of St. Peter and St. Paul, October 12, 1992).

Listen to the Voices of Creation: From Martin Palmer, "Listen to the Voices of Creation" in *Advent and Ecology; Resources for Worship, Reflection and Action*, ed. Martin Palmer and Anne Nash (ICOREC), 1988. Copyright © 1988 by Martin Palmer, World Wide Fund for Nature UK/International Consultancy on Religion, Education and Culture (ICOREC). Used by generous permission.

Litany of the Four Elements: From Kate Compston, "Litany of the Four Elements" in *Bread for Tomorrow: Praying for the World's Poor*, ed. Janet Morley (London: SPCK/Christian Aid, 1992), 176–178. Copyright © 1992 by Kate Compston (via SPCK/Christian Aid). Used by generous permission.

A Litany of Sorrow: From a service, *EASI Interfaith Celebration of the Cosmic Story* (Washington, D.C., September 12, 1993).

We Join with the Earth and Each Other: From United Nations Environmental Program, 1990. Used by permission of the United Nations Environmental Program.

A Litany of Thanksgiving for the Americas: From "A Litany of Thanksgiving for the Americas and Their People," in a service, 1492–1992: *A Celebration of Native American Survival* (Washington, D.C.: Cathedral Church of St. Peter and St. Paul, October 12, 1992).

We Live in Relation to All Things: From a service, *EASI Interfaith Celebration of the Cosmic Story* (Washington, D.C.,

September 12, 1993).

Let the Light Fall Warm and Red on the Rock: From Alison Newall, "A Creation Liturgy" (original title), *The Iona Community Worship Book* (Glasgow: Wild Goose Publications, 1991). Used by permission.

For Coconuts and Taro: From *Litany of Praise from the Pacific* (original title), source unknown. Adapted by Anne Rowthorn.

The Trees Shall Clap Their Hands: From *A Litany for the Environment* (original title), (Mutuma, Kirinyaqa, Kenya: Trinity Church, May 19, 1991).

Restore Our Earth Household: From "Earth Rebirth," *The Covenant of Peace: A Liberation Prayer Book* (The Free Church of Berkeley), ed. John Pairman Brown and Richard L. York (New York: Morehouse-Barlow, 1971), 195–197. Copyright © 1971 by The Free Church of Berkeley. Used by permission.

God of All Power: Adapted by Anne Rowthorn, *The Book of Common Prayer* (Episcopal Church) (New York: Church Hymnal Corporation, 1977), 370, and Lutheran Book of Worship (Philadelphia: Board of Publication, Lutheran Church in America), 39.

A Buddhist Litany for Peace: From Thich Nhat Hanh, *Oxford Book of Prayers* (Oxford: Oxford University Press, 1976). Reprinted by permission of Oxford University Press and The Venerable Thich Nhat Hanh.

O God of the Great Waters, Protect Us: From "To the Waters" (original title), Rig-Veda, 2nd, ed., ed. P. Lal (Calcutta, India: Writers Workshop, 1970), 21. Adapted by Anne Rowthorn. Used by permission.

In the Beginning, God Made the World: From Alison Newall, "Morning Liturgy" (original title), *A Wee Worship Book*, ed. John L. Bell (Glasgow: Wild Goose Worship Group, 1989). Copyright © 1989 by WGRG, Iona Community, 840 Govan Road, Glasgow G51 3UU, Scotland. Used by permission.

A Divine Voice Sings through All Creation: From *Gates of Prayer: The New Union Prayerbook* (New York: Central Conference of American Rabbis, 1975), 651.

Creation's Song of Praise: From "Song of the Three Young Men" in "The Apocryphal Deuterocanonical Books of the Old Testament, 35–65," *Book of Common Prayer* (Episcopal Church), 88–90 (New York: The Church Hymnal Corporation, 1977). Adaptations by Anne Rowthorn.

Praise of God's Creation in Chants and Echoes: From Metropolitan Tryphon, "An Akathist in Praise of God's Creation" (original title, 1934) in *Orthodoxy and Ecology Resource Book*, ed. Alexander Belopfpsky and Dmitiri Oikonomou (Bailystok, Poland: Orthdruk Orthodox Printing House, 1996). Adapted by Anne Rowthorn. Used by permission.

Praise to the Breath of Life: From "To the Breath of Life" (original title), Atharva-Veda, *Hindu Scriptures*, ed. and trans. R. C. Zaehner (London: J. M. Dent, 1938, 1984), 27–30, passim. Reprinted with permission from Everyman's Library, David Campbell Publishers.

From before the World Began and after the End of Eternity: From Alison Newall, *A Wee Worship Book*, ed. John L. Bell (Glasgow; Wild Goose Resource Group, 1989). Copyright © 1989 by WGRG, Iona Community, 840 Govan Road, Glasgow G51 3UU, Scotland. Used by permission.

Earth and All the Stars: An Agape Liturgy: Arranged and adapted by Anne Rowthorn from the following: "Creation Liturgy," *New Zealand Prayer Book* (Anglican Church of the Province of New Zealand: William Collins Publishers, 1989), 456–473. *Book-He Karakia Mihinare o Aotearoa* and is used with permission; "Creation Creed," *Maryknoll Magazine* (March, 1993). Reprinted and used by permission of *Maryknoll Magazine;* D. Pedro Casaldaliga,

Jaci C. Maraschin, and Milton Nascimento, "The prayer at the offering" (Misa dos Quilombros), in *A Brazilian Liturgy of Creation*, Ernesto Cardoso and Marcos Gianelli (Geneva: World Council of Churches, 1989), 74. Arrangement and adaptations © 1999 Anne Rowthorn.

CHAPTER 5: BLESSINGS

The Blessing of Light: From "An Old Irish Blessing" (original title), author unknown, *All Year Round* (London: British Council of Churches, 1987). Used by permission.

The White Sun Has Sunk Beyond the Hills: From Wang Tsu-huan, "The Sun Has Sunk Beyond the Hills," *The Four Seasons of T'ang Poetry* ed. John C. H. Wu (Rutland, Vt. and Tokyo, Japan; Charles E. Tuttle, 1972). Used by permission of Charles E. Tuttle Co., Inc., of Boston, Massachusetts and Tokyo, Japan.

Creator Spirit: From the Brothers of Weston Priory, "Prayer of Blessing, 1" (original title), *Hear the Song of Your People: Morning and Evening at Weston Priory* (Weston, Vermont: The Benedictine Foundation, 1998). Copyright © 1998 by The Benedictine Foundation of the State of Vt., Inc. Used by generous permission.

May the Ice Blanket Spread Out: Author unknown. From Ruth L. Bunzel in "Introduction to Zuñi Ceremonialism," *Forty-Seventh Annual Report of the Bureau of Zuñi American Ethnology*, 1929–1930 (Washington, D.C., 1932), 484.

Peace Be to Earth and Airy Space: From Atharva-Veda, XIX. Source of translation unknown. Adapted by Anne Rowthorn.

As the Earth Keeps Turning: From *Let's Worship*, vol. 11, (Geneva: Risk Books, World Council of Churches, 1975), 25. Copyright © 1975 by World Council of Churches, Geneva, Switzerland. Used by permission.

Benedicitio: From Edward Abbey, *Earth Apples: The Poetry of Edward Abbey*, ed. David Peterson (New York: St. Martin's Press, 1994), 110. Copyright ©1994 by St. Martin's Press, LLC. Reprinted by permission of St. Martin's Press, LLC.

FINAL EPIGRAPH

From T. S. Eliot, "Little Gidding," *Four Quartets* (New York: Harcourt, 1942). Copyright © 1942 by T. S. Eliot and renewed by Esme Valerie Eliot. Reprinted by permission of Harcourt, Inc.

ABOUT THE AUTHOR

photo by Jeffrey Rowthorn

Anne Rowthorn is a passionate environmentalist who has spent most of her life working for causes that promote peace and justice on this planet. She was born in Boston, Massachusetts and has lived in New England, New York, London, and Paris. She has a Ph.D. from New York University and is the author of five books, including *Caring for Creation* (Morehouse Publishing), a book about the environmental crisis.

Because of her husband's position as an international church leader, Dr. Rowthorn lives part of the year in a small rural town in eastern Connecticut and the rest of the time in a historic quarter of Paris. Currently she teaches at the Hartford Seminary in Connecticut, a post-graduate educational institution seeking to serve God by supporting faithful living in a multi-faith and pluralistic world. Soon she will begin research on a new book on ecological spirituality.

Anne and her husband, Jeffery, are the parents of a daughter and two sons.

A WORD ABOUT GREENPEACE

Greenpeace was born off the coast of Alaska on September 15, 1971, when a rectangular green sail carrying peace and ecology symbols was hoisted above the *Phyllis Cormack*, an aging halibut seiner which had been rented for the voyage and renamed *Greenpeace*. It was en route to Amchitka, the nuclear test island in the Aleutians, where its twelve crew members were going to protest nuclear tests in one of the most earthquake-prone regions of the world. In making the journey they said, "Our goal is very simple... insisting upon conserving the environment for our children and for future generations."

Thus began Greenpeace's commitment to direct action, non-violent public campaigns with the goal of transforming our understanding of the world and the direction in which it is heading. Throughout the years, the message has remained the same — everyone has a right to clean water, fresh air, and a safe future. For almost thirty years Greenpeace has been a force behind the enactment of virtually every national law and international convention concerning the environment.

Now with a campaign presence in forty countries and the ability to mobilize quickly in any region of the world, Greenpeace seeks to protect our fragile earth through action in the following areas: oceans, forests, climate change, nuclear issues, toxics, and genetic engineering.

Campaigns in these areas reflect Greenpeace's passion to preserve the natural world which sustains all life and nourishes and inspires the human spirit. I am very pleased to be dedicating half of my royalties from this book to help Greenpeace continue this important work. If you would like more information about Greenpeace, please contact your regional Greenpeace office or:

Greenpeace USA
1436 U Street, N.W.
Washington, DC 20009
USA
Telephone: (202) 462-1177
Fax: (202) 462-4507
E-mail: greenpeace.usa@wdc.greenpeace.org

Greenpeace International
Keizersgracht 176
1016 DW Amsterdam
The Netherlands
Telephone: (31) 20-523-6222
Fax: (31) 20-523-6200
E-mail: supporterservices@ams.greenpeace.org

Web site address: www.greenpeace.org

If you enjoyed *Earth and All the Stars* we highly recommend the following books:

Animal Grace by Mary Lou Randour. As well as a call to action, *Animal Grace* is a book of stories about how both domestic and wild animals have helped people heal from illness, cope with death, and learn to love. Randour devotes several chapters to how the world's religions approach human relationships with animals, and she offers comprehensive directions on how to enter and deepen reciprocal relationships with other species.

The Sacred Earth edited by Jason Gardner. Drawn from the great works of contemporary American nature writing, this profound and beautiful collection of 145 quotations of poetic prose from more than 60 of our finest nature writers celebrates the earth and explores our spiritual relationship with nature.

Wonders of Solitude edited by Dale Salwak. This volume of quotations on the essential importance of solitude helps bring contemplation and silence back into our busy lives. It contains more than 300 inspiring and diverse quotations on the nature, importance, and power of solitude. *The Wonders of Solitude* is an uplifting companion in the struggle to remove ourselves, as Salwak writes, from "our peripheral concerns, from the pressures of a madly active world, and to return to the center where life is sacred — a humble miracle and mystery."

New World Library publishes books and other
forms of communication on the leading edge
of personal and planetary evolution.

Our books and audio and video cassettes
are in bookstores everywhere.
For a catalog of our complete library
of publications, contact:

New World Library
14 Pamaron Way
Novato, CA 94949

Telephone: (415) 884-2100
Fax: (415) 884-2199
Toll free: (800) 972-6657
Catalog requests: Ext. 50
Ordering: Ext. 52

E-mail: escort@nwlib.com
Web site: www.nwlib.com